T0000820

THE WAY
OF
NAGOMI

ALSO BY KEN MOGI

Awakening Your Ikigai

THE WAY
OF
NAGOMI

THE JAPANESE PHILOSOPHY
OF FINDING BALANCE AND PEACE
IN EVERYTHING YOU DO

———

KEN MOGI

THE EXPERIMENT

NEW YORK

THE WAY OF NAGOMI: *The Japanese Philosophy of Finding Balance and Peace in Everything You Do*
Copyright © 2022 by Ken Mogi
Illustrations copyright © 2022 by Amber Anderson

Originally published in the UK as *The Way of Nagomi: Live a Balanced and Harmonious Life the Japanese Way* by Quercus in 2022. First published in North America in revised form by The Experiment, LLC, in 2023.

All rights reserved. Except for brief passages quoted in newspaper, magazine, radio, television, or online reviews, no portion of this book may be reproduced, distributed, or transmitted in any form or by any means, electronic or mechanical, including photocopying, recording, or information storage or retrieval system, without the prior written permission of the publisher.

The Experiment, LLC
220 East 23rd Street, Suite 600
New York, NY 10010-4658
theexperimentpublishing.com

This book contains the opinions and ideas of its authors. It is intended to provide helpful and informative material on the subjects addressed in the book. It is sold with the understanding that the authors and publisher are not engaged in rendering medical, health, or any other kind of personal professional services in the book. The authors and publisher specifically disclaim all responsibility for any liability, loss, or risk—personal or otherwise—that is incurred as a consequence, directly or indirectly, of the use and application of any of the contents of this book.

THE EXPERIMENT and its colophon are registered trademarks of The Experiment, LLC. Many of the designations used by manufacturers and sellers to distinguish their products are claimed as trademarks. Where those designations appear in this book and The Experiment was aware of a trademark claim, the designations have been capitalized.

The Experiment's books are available at special discounts when purchased in bulk for premiums and sales promotions as well as for fundraising or educational use. For details, contact us at info@theexperimentpublishing.com.

Library of Congress Cataloging-in-Publication Data available upon request

ISBN 978-1-61519-869-6
Ebook ISBN 978-1-61519-870-2

Cover and text design by Beth Bugler
Author photograph by Itaru Hirama

Manufactured in the United States of America

First printing January 2023
10 9 8 7 6 5 4 3 2 1

CONTENTS

Introduction

As you can see from the title, this is a book about nagomi. To explain this concept, I will refer to Japanese culture, history, and people in depth, but that is not to say it is an exclusively Japanese way of thinking. Japan has traditionally been open to influences from the outside world; because it is an island nation and of relatively small size, it has imported many external cultural influences with curiosity and zeal. Historically, Chinese influence has been crucial, and those of the Korean peninsula have also been pivotal in nurturing and enriching Japanese culture. Since the nineteenth century, Japan has eagerly absorbed Western culture, too.

The evolution of society is an interconnected and continuous process. In fact, the Japanese have always regarded society as constantly changing, ephemeral, and flexible. We even have a word for it—*ukiyo* (meaning "floating world")—that beautifully illustrates this philosophy. The floating world refers to the importance of the ephemeral in Japanese life, like the appreciation of cherry blossoms in the *hanami* festivities in spring, which last only for a few days in their prime. The concept of nagomi, which has developed in Japan in its own unique way, will have similar equivalents in other parts of the world and is certainly not exclusive to Japan in terms of its roots and implications. This very process of cultural assimilation demonstrates nagomi in action, as Japanese culture has sought harmony between indigenous and imported elements.

There are also many different possible interpretations of nagomi among the Japanese people. I have tried my best to present a balanced and comprehensive picture of nagomi, but of course, other people might have different opinions. Nagomi is all about the blend and balance of different factors, so I have tried to mirror the very concept of nagomi in my description of it in this book.

As you read, you will see that nagomi enables you to achieve the following five pillars:

1. Maintain happy relationships with your loved ones, even if you disagree with them.

2. Learn new things while always staying true to yourself.

3. Find a sense of peace in whatever you are doing.

4. Mix and blend unlikely components to strike a harmonious balance.

5. Have a greater understanding of the Japanese philosophy of life.

After spending some time contemplating nagomi, I hope you can return to your own life with some fresh insights into what constitutes a happy and creative life, in harmony with other people, nature, and, finally and perhaps most importantly, yourself. If you have so far lived a life far from nagomi, that is quite all right. While the concept of nagomi has been uniquely nurtured and developed in Japan, it is relevant for everybody in today's world. You can construct a nagomi with your own life and start the way of nagomi (*nagomido*) right here, after you close this book.

Now, it's time to get started. Welcome to nagomi.

CHAPTER 1

Nagomi for Beginners

There are many different pathways to a successful, creative, and happy life. Some people get ahead by being assertive, controversial, and occasionally disruptive. Others are more enigmatic. They might be very reserved, are unlikely to trumpet their own merits, and rarely criticize other people. Despite their lack of self-assertion, however, they turn out to be excellent achievers. Their track record in life blows your mind, and yet, boasting is the last thing these people do.

There is something about the Japanese mode of living that avoids outright confrontation, even when trying to bring about innovation. For sure, there are an abundance of Japanese success stories. You don't have to look far for examples: Sony, Toyota, Honda, and Nissan—all originating in the land of the rising sun—are just a few of the great companies that have defined the postwar economy. And yet, Japanese people are famous for keeping a low profile. They are typically unassuming, gracious in defeat, and reserved in victory. They do not speak out their opinions—to the point that some people find the silence uncomfortable. It appears that the Japanese have achieved many miraculous things without necessarily asserting their own merits.

However, behind the silence and reserve of the Japanese is a long-kept secret for finding wellness and harmony within one's life. This book is about this path to personal fulfillment and peace of mind.

Let us begin with the small print. Most self-help books promise to make you happy, wealthy, or successful, or sometimes all three. Indeed, many of these books equate happiness with wealth and success. Unlike them, this book is not about finding shortcuts to happiness, success, or wealth; it is about understanding and enhancing the good and positive aspects of our lives to balance the difficulties that inevitably befall every one of us. It is about maximizing the value of our positive traits, good fortune, and success as a way of increasing our well-being and making us more resilient. This resilience enables us to cope with the bad things in life. The key is recognizing that unpleasant things are always part of life, and that the balance of the good, the bad, and everything in-between makes our lives richer and more substantial. Just as some sourness or bitterness help enhance the flavors of some dishes, so overcoming hardship can make us appreciate the good qualities present in our lives.

What is the secret? The answer can be summarized in just one word: nagomi.

If you have never heard of this word, it is not your fault. Even if you know a lot about other cultures, it is quite likely that you have never come across nagomi before. This venerable word and concept, although central to what Japan and Japanese people stand for, has been the best-kept secret of the Japanese approach to work and life for a very long time.

This is the first book—to the best of the author's knowledge—to bring nagomi to the rest of the world. It will explore the concept of nagomi, its relevance in contemporary life, as well as the historical and cultural backgrounds of nagomi, while putting it in a modern context.

But first, what is nagomi? Roughly, it means balance, comfort, and calm of the heart and mind. Nagomi could be about one's relationship with the environment, or the quality of one's communication with other people. Nagomi may be about a well-mixed and balanced blending of materials, as in the case of cooking. Nagomi can also be about one's general state of mind, as when one is in harmony with oneself and the world at large. Ultimately, nagomi is a state of human consciousness characterized by a sense of ease, emotional balance, well-being, and calmness. Crucially, nagomi assumes that there are different elements to begin with, not just a unified and coherent whole. In kanji (the Japanese version of Chinese characters), it shares the same Chinese character (和) as *wa*, meaning "harmony."

Semantically speaking, the verb *nagomu* is an intransitive verb, and it represents the spontaneous act of coming to a state of nagomi. The transitive verb *nagomaseru*, on the other hand, describes the active process of putting a few elements together and creating a harmonious whole. In daily usage, the verbs *nagomu* and *nagomaseru* together are concerned with providing relief

from conditions of stress, tension, discord, or concern, which are unfortunately the hallmarks of contemporary life in Japan and elsewhere. The word *nagomi* is also related to the word *nagi*, which describes the calm of the sea. In some contexts, nagi (calm sea) can be a symbol of tranquility and peace.

Nagomi, as a word representing all these detailed, subtle, and rich nuances, defies a simple equivalent English translation. Its meaning changes slightly in each specific context, so throughout this book, I will go through the different aspects of nagomi to show how it applies in all areas of life.

Because of its positive connotations, nagomi is a popular term in Japan. Restaurants, nursing homes, green tea brands, ice cream flavors, hot springs, wedding planning companies, *shinrin-yoku* (forest bathing) services, a spa in a luxury hotel, an orchestra, and a computer font all boast the name nagomi. Nagomi is also the name of a special train reserved for the emperor only. The nagomi train is constructed with the latest technology and greatest care, characteristic of the Japanese people. The train surface is painted dark purple, a color traditionally considered to be of aristocratic nature, and is polished to a mirrorlike effect. Details of the design of the imperial carriage itself are not known, and the train itself is off-limits most of the time. On select occasions, however, the general public does have the opportunity to ride the nagomi train on specially designed tours, and reviews of such trips invariably declare how wonderful a train it is. The fact that nagomi is used as the name for this highest quality train is a testimony that nagomi is regarded highly in Japanese cultural and historical traditions.

Nagomi is not about tradition alone. It continues to evolve as Japan opens its doors more and more to the outside world. For example, it is the name of a home visit program for tourists from abroad, where registered Japanese households welcome international visitors, cooking for them so that they may all enjoy time spent dining together in their homes.

Nagomi is considered to be the mother of important concepts such as *wabi sabi*, Zen, *kintsugi*, *ichigo ichie*, and *ikigai*. Indeed, it is not an overstatement to say that nagomi is at the pinnacle of Japanese culture and central to the Japanese philosophy of life. The almost sublime importance of nagomi can be traced back in records to the Seventeen Articles Constitution drafted by Prince Shotoku in the year 604, believed to be the first constitution of Japan as a nation. The first article proclaims that "WA is important," using the Chinese and more formal representation of the concept of nagomi, which suggests that Japan is a nation built on the concept of nagomi.

Nagomi is related to wellness of mind, but you can find nagomi even if you aren't very happy. The beauty of nagomi is that it helps one to come to terms with a perceived lack of happiness or even occasional disaster. It can help us to accept certain situations, even if they are not ideal. This might sound confusing, but I'll explain how nagomi can offer many ways to live a more stress-free, relaxed, and resilient life. And the best news is that it can help anyone—whoever you are and wherever you come from.

I'm excited to introduce you to the concept of nagomi, the heart of every important aspect of the Japanese philosophy of life.

Let us now begin the journey of nagomi.

CHAPTER 2

Nagomi of Food

Let's dive in with a tangible example of nagomi: eating.

Japan is famous for its creative use of food materials. It has always been world-leading in terms of its cuisine, which is balanced both in terms of pleasure and in its promotion of good health.

Nagomi is at the center of the philosophy and technique of Japanese cooking, and is particularly exemplified by *kaiseki*, which describes the balance of ingredients in dishes. Kaiseki is about appreciating the various blessings of nature, and nagomi in this context is the umbrella term that describes this Japanese approach to harmony in food.

In the western suburb of Japan's ancient capital Kyoto lies the Arashiyama region, famous for its breathtakingly beautiful paths among bamboo trees and tranquil temples. By the side of the Oigawa River, near the Moon Crossing Bridge (Togetsukyo), you can find the three-Michelin-starred restaurant Arashiyama Kitcho. It is proudly headed by the chef Kunio Tokuoka, a grandson of Teiichi Yuki, and if you are ever lucky enough to secure a reservation at this world-famous restaurant, brace yourself for true culinary art. Yuki was the first ever culinary professional to be presented with the medal of Person of Cultural Merit by the Japanese government, for his efforts in modernizing the concept of kaiseki. He is considered to be the godfather of Japan's modern kaiseki tradition, which is now regarded as one of the most important culinary achievements in the world.

The kaiseki cuisine comes from the great tradition of the Japanese tea ceremony and is a perfect example of the practical application of nagomi. It is all about the harmony between various sensory elements: first pleasing your eyes with a delicately arranged choreography of materials, and then delighting your tongue with exquisite flavors. Kaiseki is achieved when ingredients and materials are taken from all corners of the land and sea and put together in a harmonious whole, with appealing colors and forms of display, reflecting a deep appreciation of the seasonality that is so typical of Japan.

Once, Kenichiro Nishi, the famous chef at the sublime Kyoaji restaurant in Tokyo, confided to me that the secret of his mastery was taking the seasons seriously. In Japan, perception of the seasons is very nuanced, with special words used to describe the different phases of seasons. *Hashiri* refers to the start of the season, when the new ingredients start to fill the market. *Nagori* is the end of the season, when the ingredients become less and less available. Hashiri and nagori are both highly prized and anticipated by connoisseurs, and the relevant ingredients go for incredibly high retail prices.

However, Nishi told me that ingredients are actually at their tastiest when they are right in the middle of the season (*sakari*). At this stage, they are available in large quantities and so the prices are lower. Nishi told me that the job of a Japanese chef is not to make a fuss about scarce ingredients and charge customers scandalous prices for them, but rather to make the most of ingredients when they are abundant. Kaiseki—although sometimes very steeply priced—is actually a simple affair involving the most common ingredients from land and sea. It is a humble and yet creative mixing of things taken from nature, a dedication of one's skills to what is readily available. Kaiseki is an attitude as much as a genre of cooking, and simple everyday Japanese cooking can still embody the spirit of nagomi.

Almost all dishes in Japan are an *okazu* (accompaniment) to rice. If you stay at a Japanese-style inn (*ryokan*), typically for breakfast you will be served a variety of dishes, including pickles, nori (seaweed), roasted fish, marinated vegetables, seasoned meat, and natto (fermented soybeans), along with the ubiquitous and almost compulsory rice and miso soup. Most of the items on a Japanese breakfast table are prepared in such a way that they taste extremely good when mixed and consumed along with rice. In other words, these dishes are at their optimum when eaten with rice.

Kids in Japan are instructed by their parents to take mouthfuls of rice and okazu in turn when eating breakfast, so they can experience the best possible flavor sensations. It is common to put more than one okazu in the mouth at one time, together with the rice, so that you taste a variety of ingredients simultaneously. This practice, called *kounaichoumi* (cooking in the mouth), is a wonderfully physical embodiment of nagomi. No taste is an island entirely on its own. When cooking and consuming with nagomi, two things do not have a battle in your mouth. It's about mixing the flavors so they become one on your tongue, and achieving the utmost harmony possible in your eating experience.

The famous Japanese bento box is a visual expression of the method used to achieve kounaichoumi and the philosophy of nagomi behind it. A typical bento features a portion of rice, often in a square shape, together with several other items, all arranged neatly like pieces in a puzzle. There is no main dish; everything is offered in neat small portions and is designed to go well with the rice. As long as they achieve nagomi with rice, it does not really matter how many different items there are in the bento box. There is an even more elegantly presented bento, called *shokado*, which has a deep connection with the kaiseki spirit. It originated in the Shokado house and gardens in the southern suburb of Kyoto and has become synonymous with refined cuisine presented in a bento format. Many upmarket restaurants offer shokado bento for customers who are in a hurry and want to eat quickly, or for takeout.

Bento making in Japan has always been a serious affair. It is not about just putting some sandwiches and an apple in a brown paper bag, as would be typical in some parts of the world. We make such a fuss about it, there are even books dedicated to the art of bento making.

The most essential principle is to prepare various items in small portions. Rice is always at the center, unifying the other items. You can replace rice with the staples available in your local supermarket, such as bread, pasta, tortillas, potatoes, couscous, or polenta. If you prepare a variety of food items in small portions and arrange them with rice or your staple starch of choice, then you have reproduced the essence of kaiseki or shokado. All you need to do now is to realize nagomi through your kounai-choumi (cooking in the mouth)!

Not only does food arranged in such a way look good, but the kaiseki and bento formats also exemplify several principles and benefits of the nagomi approach and the kounaichoumi method of consumption. For one, they both help achieve the all-important nutritional balance. Second, they provide the chef with many opportunities to showcase their skills in one sitting. Third, the sheer diversity of the ingredients provides a great chance to represent the various blessings we receive from nature, making this typically Japanese cuisine resonant with the environment we live in.

However, this approach to food often bewilders people from the regions where these ingredients actually originated. One intriguing example is gyoza.

Gyoza dumplings, which originated in China, are now ubiquitous in Japan. Restaurants specializing in gyoza are becoming popular, with one restaurant proudly proclaiming that "gyoza and beer are one culture together," which is one of my favorite slogans. Outside Japan, gyoza have come to represent a staple part of Japanese cuisine. It might surprise you, then, when I say that the way gyoza are prepared and consumed in Japan is totally different from that in their country of origin. And this has much to do with nagomi, and kounaichoumi in particular.

I once had a friendly argument with a Chinese couple on a cruise ship. No, we were not debating to which country some disputed islands belonged. We were discussing whether it was acceptable to eat gyoza together with rice—that is to say, as *okazu*. The Chinese couple were adamant. It was inconceivable, they said. They even suggested that it was sacrilegious. Gyoza were gyoza, they said, and should be eaten by themselves, and never with rice. They even suggested that it made them feel ill to think that there would be people on the planet who were senseless enough to eat gyoza with rice.

"But gyoza are so great," I protested. "You know in Japanese restaurants, gyoza and rice is such a popular dish. You dip the gyoza in spicy soy sauce and eat it with rice. . . . Yum! It's so tasty."

The Chinese couple looked astonished, as if they were talking to a barbarian.

"That may be so. . . . There is no accounting for taste. But we think it is gross to eat gyoza with rice."

So, no matter how friendly the conversation was, we could not come to a mutual agreement on this one.

To be precise, the gyoza consumed in China are mainly *suigyoza* (boiled dumplings), which are cooked in hot water and added to a tasty soup. Suigyoza have a soft and moist casing. The gyoza popular in Japan are *yakigyoza* (pan-fried gyoza), with a crisp casing and juicy meat or vegetables inside. Even in Japan, it is perhaps not that typical to eat rice with suigyoza, although some people do that (myself included). Eating yakigyoza with rice, though, is a very popular custom in Japan. I myself love yakigyoza with rice, where you dip the yakigyoza in spicy soy sauce and eat them with white steamed rice. (Writing this makes my mouth water. . . .) It is interesting to observe that gyoza started to evolve in a direction that meant they would be tastier when consumed with rice, rather than eaten by themselves. This is a very typical application of the principle of nagomi (better together, in this context) to this venerable Chinese dish.

The concept of nagomi in the practice of kounaichoumi encourages us to incorporate and embrace many different materials from nature, from the mountains to the sea. The same spirit is true of the Japanese tradition of consuming many different kinds of food with sake—rice wine—Japan's hallmark alcoholic drink.

An *izakaya* is a Japanese tavern offering alcoholic drinks and food, and it has a long history; it dates back at least to the beginning of the eighth century. In the film masterpieces of the director Akira Kurosawa, such as *Yojimbo* and *Sanjuro*, you can see samurai, most memorably played by the great Japanese actor Toshiro Mifune in his roles as Sanjuro Kuwabatake and Sanjuro Tsubaki, having a good time in an izakaya. Although a modern-day izakaya offers a wide variety of alcoholic beverages such as beer, wine, shochu, and whisky, sake

remains the central and most important drink. Indeed, sake is the defining drink in an izakaya.

There are many options on the menu in an izakaya, but the staples are sashimi, edamame, marinated vegetables, tofu, *yakitori*, roast pork, and *yakisoba* noodles. Although the dishes provided by izakaya are wide-ranging, they share one thing in common: They taste extremely good when consumed with sake. In other words, they are all *tsumami*, a word that describes the range of dishes specially conceived and developed to accompany sake. Today, tsumami can also refer to food that can be accompanied by other alcoholic drinks such as beer, whisky, and wine. One can say, for example, that edamame is a perfect tsumami for beer, or that cheese is an excellent tsumami for wine. However, tsumami refers mainly to the food that goes with sake. One can say that an izakaya is a place where they provide sake and various tsumami. It is wonderful to be in an izakaya and observe the simply blissful nagomi developing in your mouth as you taste your sake with tsumami. This is again an application of kounaichoumi. Here, sake is the finishing touch to the tsumami, which are tasty in their own right.

In the western part of Japan, the word *ate* (pronounced as in the French word *pâté*) often replaces tsumami. The fact that it has the same spelling as the past tense of "eat" is purely coincidental, but it makes it easier to remember that if you go to an izakaya in Osaka, you would ask for sake and *ate* instead of sake and tsumami. In earlier times, there was the word *sakana*, which described any kind of food that was good with sake. Etymologically, sakana derives from the combination of "sake" and *na*, the latter describing any subsidiary ingredients or dishes that accompanied the main flavor (sake, in this case). Thus, anything that accompanied sake was considered to be sakana. Interestingly, in modern Japanese, sakana is also the umbrella term to describe various kinds of fish. This does make sense, since fish dishes, most notably sashimi, go wonderfully well with sake. And since in modern Japanese, sakana has come to refer primarily to fish, people tend to use tsumami (or *ate*) to describe the culinary delights that accompany sake.

The goodness of okazu or tsumami is defined in relation to rice or sake. Of course, sake is made from rice, so the fact that other foods are measured according to their performance with rice and sake is a testimony to rice's status as an important crop in Japan. Indeed, it is *the most* important crop, so much so that the emperor himself ceremonially plants rice every year in the Imperial Palace. Historically, the area of land designated for a samurai warrior was measured in terms of the size of the rice crop the land had produced.

On a more philosophical level, rice and sake are also symbolic of the values associated with the ideal of nagomi. The best quality rice and sake are marked by their neutrality, lack of self-assertion, and their remarkable ability to mix well with various other flavors and ingredients, which are likely to be more colorful and conspicuous compared to the seemingly humble rice and sake themselves. It can even be said that the Japanese ideal of the self in society is something like a good rice or sake, a far cry from more self-asserting personalities. Perhaps that is why Japanese people tend to think it is fitting that the emperor, who is always reserved and unassuming, should plant rice every year. It is also considered apt to offer rice and sake to gods at a Shinto shrine, reflecting the notion that neutrality is resonant, in this context to the point of being suitable for religious or spiritual purposes.

However, rice and sake aren't alone in representing the ultimate shrine of nagomi. There is a wide range of food that embodies the spirit of nagomi, and dishes such as ramen, katsu curry, and *oyako don* could all be considered the result of attempts to find nagomi between Japan's indigenous cooking culture and influences from abroad.

Over the years, we in Japan have developed a taste for many different cooking styles imported from all over the world. The Japanese expression *wayochu* refers to the cooking styles originating in Japan (*wa*), the West (*yo*), and China (*chu*), and it represents the major genres of foods available in modern Japan. Today, almost all over Japan, no matter how small the town is, you are able to find restaurants serving selections of *wayochu* items, typically focusing on one of the three genres, but in some cases serving all of them. Indeed, Western cuisine is so ubiquitous in Japan that people often joke that "the best French cooking is to be found in Japan."

Katsu curry might be one of the Japanese dishes that has found the most rapid and international reception. This is particularly true, in my experience anyway, of the UK. I have visited England regularly since I did my post-doc in Cambridge, over two decades ago. It has been interesting to see how Japanese cooking has come to be so widely accepted in that once gastronomically conservative country. I can still recall my shock when, as I was having lunch in a sushi restaurant in Victoria station almost a decade ago, a British person ordered "katsu curry." I had never expected this beloved Japanese dish to travel so far. Only a few years later, as I was walking down one of the busiest streets in central London, I noticed a billboard proclaiming that the restaurant it advertised had "the best katsu curry in town." When you consider how katsu curry originated, you appreciate how it is a beautiful example of the nagomi principle at work. The habit of eating meat was only introduced to Japan through the influence of modernization from the West, and curry of course comes from India. Thus, katsu curry stands for a mixture of many different influences from all over the world, blending all in one harmonious whole—a beautiful example of the nagomi of food.

Ramen is another interesting example of nagomi. It originated in China, but now people from all over the world flock to the ramen noodle shops in Japan. The universe of ramen has expanded, and there are many bewildering varieties. In Tokyo, you can sample soups based on salt, soy sauce, miso, fish, pork bone marrow, chicken bones, vegetables, and so on. The variety of noodles and toppings is also wide-ranging. The sky, or rather, your imagination, is the limit. There are no taboos, as long as it all tastes good. In other words, everything is possible as long as the ingredients are in nagomi.

As Japanese people are typically used to applying kounaichoumi from childhood, there are relatively few psychological barriers when it comes to putting unusual ingredients together. This principle of free association has helped the universe of Japanese cuisine expand. Nagomi makes almost anything possible.

Perhaps the best-known result of the culinary flexibility afforded by nagomi is sushi. Sushi is an incredibly fluid food style. Take maki (roll), for example. There are several traditional maki styles, and the fine restaurants in Tokyo stick to them. If you go into one of these establishments and ask for a nontraditional maki, all you would get might be a frown. However, the rest of the world is entirely free to deviate from those gatekeepers of tradition. In fact, it is possible to prepare maki in many different ways, such as the California roll, caterpillar roll, and the Alaska roll, but you won't find these varieties easily in Japan. Americans might find it disappointing that California rolls, for example, are hard to come by in Tokyo's established restaurants. And although crazily popular outside Japan, ordering salmon in a fine sushi restaurant is one sure way to get a disdainful look from the chef behind the counter, as salmon is not considered to be an authentic fish to be used in a traditional sushi, owing partly to the fact that most of it is imported from outside Japan. The sushi style in Tokyo and elsewhere in Japan has remained largely unchanged, to the joy of the purists and visitors in the know. However, once you are outside the jealously guarded traditional sushi circle, you are entirely free to do whatever you might want, as long as what you do is nagomi. You could come up with the craziest recipe and it would still be sushi. Making playfully innovative sushi resonates with what the Japanese have been doing in the spirit of nagomi over the years.

At *kaiten sushi* (rotating sushi) restaurants in Japan, you sit at the table, and the rotating belt carries past you dishes featuring a variety of food on small plates. Everything is possible and readily accepted. There might even be sweet sushi topped with cream and chocolate, or pieces incorporating Western dishes, such as roast beef sushi. Needless to say, you can get salmon in a *kaiten sushi*; in fact, salmon sushi is one of the most popular dishes in these restaurants.

Sushi is a wonderful application of the spirit of nagomi, in which elements of many different cultural origins can be blended into a tasty whole. The secret of the great flexibility of sushi can be found, again, in rice. This ubiquitous, white, and steaming grain is at the heart of the nagomi of Japanese cooking. Without rice, nagomi in cuisine would be impossible. Indeed, rice is the apotheosis of nagomi in cooking. Because of the adaptability of rice, the Japanese people have been able to welcome many influences from abroad.

Although katsu curry and roast beef sushi might be available outside Japan, if you don't live in Japan, it may be difficult to appreciate the whole spectrum of nagomi in Japanese cooking. Menus based on the nagomi principles are endless and new ones are constantly being invented. It can take a while for these culinary innovations to catch on more widely. This is changing, however, and now nagomi can even come bottled.

The Japanese whisky brand Suntory is one such example. Seiichi Koshimizu, who has been the chief blender at the company for many years, developed his approach by recognizing the unique properties of every single malt stored in his company's barrels. His application of fresh insight to each stage of the unpredictable nature of the maturing process helped Japanese whisky come to the forefront in the global market both in terms of quality and prestige. Today, the main brands of Suntory whisky, many of which have a kanji (Japanese version of Chinese characters) name such as *Hibiki* or *Hakushu*, are so popular that the company asks its employees not to drink its whisky; there is insufficient quantity to meet the demand from all over the world. This ingenuity also explains why Japanese craft gins are increasingly popular—something that took me by surprise one day.

A great friend of mine, Dan Ruderman, once emailed me from his home in California. Dan boasted that he had been enjoying a Japanese gin, Kinobi, which he believed to be one of the best in the world. To be honest, I had not heard of Kinobi, or even the concept of Japanese craft gin, until that day. Dan described how fragrant and refreshingly rich Kinobi was. I immediately believed him, whom I knew to be a person of good taste. A few weeks later, I was enjoying some wine in a bar in Tokyo. I remembered Dan's words, and casually asked the bartender if he had Kinobi. He said yes and brought me one. What I tasted then was truly an eye-opener. The transparent liquid in the glass tasted like nothing I'd had before.

Kinobi, which is produced at the Kyoto Distillery in Japan's ancient capital, is a beautiful example of what the principle of nagomi can accomplish. As in the case of the great Suntory whiskies, it is the balance between the different elements that makes this gin so special. The official page of the Kyoto Distillery boasts eleven botanicals (juniper berry, orris, hinoki, yuzu, lemon, *gyokuro* green tea, ginger, red shiso leaves, bamboo leaves, *sansho* pepper, and *kinome*) in six flavor groups (base, citrus, tea, spice, fruity and floral, and herbal). Of this plethora of ingredients, yuzu, a special kind of citrus fruit with a distinct flavor that is ubiquitous in Japanese cooking—and is becoming quite common in cooking overseas, too—is perhaps the most important and defining feature. Intriguingly, these botanicals (yuzu, gyokuro green tea, sansho pepper, and kinome, in particular) are routinely used in Japanese cooking, including in the sublime dishes of kaiseki.

During the assimilation of external influences after the modernization of Japan in the nineteenth century, many uniquely Japanese forms of nagomi—including whiskey, gins, katsu curry, oyako don, gyoza, and ramen—sprang up. All of this came out of efforts to accommodate external influences in creative ways. The most striking insight to be gained from this is that nagomi is perhaps the single most important guiding principle of Japanese cuisine. When a nagomi between the ingredients is achieved, the dish tastes good, often heavenly.

Here are some of the ways nagomi is applied to food making:

One, when cooking add ingredients without prejudice, no matter what the origin of them might be, both culturally and geographically. The nagomi of food is a very liberal attitude.

Two, blend and mix them, and try to strike a balance between the different ingredients without overriding them with a strong sauce, no matter how tasty or effective it might be. Thus, Japanese food is famous for its meticulous care and consideration of each food item on its own merit, rather than directing and forcing it into a particular taste. The nagomi of food is democratic.

Three, through the nagomi of mixing and blending, some new flavors and textures are born, often with unexpected and surprising results. The nagomi of food is a creative process. Matcha ice cream, which blends ice cream (a food item of Western origin) with matcha (powdered tea leaves, a uniquely Japanese botanical), is a quintessential example of the creative aspect of the nagomi of food.

Finally, *omakase* (chef's choice) is a concept in which the chef will try to strike a nagomi balance between the variety of food ingredients available on the day by carefully preparing and serving them in the right order and combinations. The assumption in Japan is that there is an asymmetry of knowledge between the customer and the chef; it is better for the chef to decide which ingredients to use and present, rather than having the customer order their own. Depending on the season, the chef will choose and prepare the best available ingredients with optimum amounts of sauces and spice, so that the customer will just have to put the food into their mouth like a carefree child. There is a nagomi of trusting relationship between the customer and the chef.

So, if you go to a good Japanese restaurant, sit at the counter, and ask for that day's omakase, you can expect everything to be prepared with a spirit of nagomi. You will feel at one with the chef who created your food, as if you are communicating with them directly. Dining in a nice Japanese restaurant should hopefully make you feel as if you are connected to the very core of this universe, and that is down to nagomi.

CHAPTER 3

Nagomi of Self

The professions we regard most highly as a society change over time. Whereas in the past, most Japanese children aspired to be professional baseball players, actors, singers, or anime directors, in recent years, surveys have shown that being a YouTuber is now one of the most aspirational occupations.

This isn't just the case in Japan. In 2020, Ryan Kaji, a twelve-year-old based in Texas, was the highest earning YouTuber in the world, having already earned $2.8 million at the tender age of nine. His channel, Ryan's World, features videos of him unboxing various toys and other items, and boasts, at my last count, 28.5 million subscribers. Given this demonstration of success and at such a scale, it is no wonder that kids look to the YouTubers for inspiration for their own careers.

Another example is Yutaka Nakamura, also known as Yutabon, who started his channel with his father's help when he was just eight years old. I vividly remember the first time I met Yutabon in Naha, the main city of the southern island of Okinawa, in 2019. Okinawa is an area identified as one of the Blue Zones of health and longevity by the American author David Buettner in his talks about *ikigai*, which, if you've read my first book, you will know is the Japanese philosophy that helps you to find mindfulness and joy in everything you do. People who live in Okinawa have some of the longest life spans in the world, with some residents living up to the incredible age of 110 years, and the good health of Okinawans is considered to be linked to both genetics and diet. Yutabon had moved to Okinawa from his hometown of Osaka the previous year, and at the time of our meeting, was not yet widely known. Yutabon's channel deals mainly with being a young person who refuses to go to school, and it didn't take long for him to become a household name.

When I met Yutabon, he talked vehemently about his indignation at the unfair ways he felt his teachers treated him. After a particularly unpleasant incident, in which a teacher refused to understand his point, Yutabon refused to go to school and instead started his own learning projects. He graduated from elementary school in March 2021 but was not allowed to participate in the general ceremony, as his hair was dyed blond. In Japan, schools typically regard black hair as the only natural or right color, and any kid who dyes their hair another color tends to find themselves in trouble. This is perhaps ridiculous when you consider that kids with a naturally lighter hair shade are sometimes told to dye their hair black.

The case of Yutabon is interesting, as it tells a universal yet unique story. It reminds us how difficult it can be to grow up in a society where there is a lot of peer pressure. At the same time, it demonstrates how it is possible to come to a state of nagomi with other people, even in a school environment where there are too many rules and too little leniency. It is wonderful to see Yutabon in a truly upbeat mood, happily learning what he wants. It's inspirational to observe Yutabon's mind at work, even from the point of view of adults.

Yutabon's story resonates with that of Naoki Higashida, the author of *The Reason I Jump: One Boy's Voice from the Silence of Autism*. In his book, Higashida describes how he overcame the difficulties of growing up in a world where the people around him did not feel and think in the same way as he did. The experiences of Yutabon and Higashida are different in that they are not just stories of the triumph of individuality, but also of the fulfillment of a nagomi with society. Their lives might not be typical, but their courageous stories provide important insights as to how we all might live. Learning to accommodate other people's differences is nagomi in action.

Many of the difficulties and challenges of the modern world are related to the problem of the self. It is a natural human tendency to compare ourselves with other people, but we too often judge ourselves in relation to the perceived values of others. There are many adages that express this concept, such as "keeping up with the Joneses" (or Kardashians), "the grass is always greener on the other side," or, as they say in Japan, "the flower next door is redder." Throughout our childhood, adolescence, and adulthood, we allow other people to be our mirror. This is normal, but it can also cause problems when it comes to nurturing and maintaining the self in the wider community. Worst of all, we often give other people, especially those close to us, the power and authority to determine the way we feel about ourselves. That almost came to pass for Yutabon in his school life, but ultimately he refused to let the teacher exert too much influence on the makeup of his personality.

In the past, the pool of people against which we compared ourselves was defined by our location and social circle, and so it was small. In recent years, social networking services such as Twitter, Facebook, Instagram, and TikTok have made it possible to compare oneself with millions of people around the globe. Some use social media as self-promotional platforms to show the world how cool, beautiful, and interesting they are. The arms race between individuals on social media has led to a situation where many feel the pressure to curate their online presence, to essentially advertise themselves. Needless to say, this does not lead to happiness most of the time—and this is where nagomi comes in.

In order to achieve satisfaction in one's life, one needs to arrive at a place of nagomi. The first step is self-acceptance. This challenge is different for everyone, because people are born into different circumstances. Evidence suggests that insufficient love and support during childhood impairs one's ability to control one's emotions in adulthood. However, this is not to suggest that what childhood experiences we have will determine and dominate our well-being in later life. It's just that some people are born into a "lucky" family background, whereas others have a rough time overcoming a troubled start in life.

Even if you are lucky with your upbringing, however, it does not automatically mean you will have natural nagomi. In the science of life satisfaction (aka happiness), a cognitive model called "focusing illusion" is known to play an important role. This describes the tendency to be too focused on a particular perceived defect or shortcoming in one's circumstances and to become unduly unsatisfied (unhappy) because of it. This means that it is possible to be unduly unhappy, even though objectively the situation is not so bad at all. A rich person might have the self-perception that they are physically unattractive; an attractive person might have had parents who undermined them; a naturally smart person may have had limited access to education. Seldom is anyone fortunate enough to have luck in all elements that contribute to a good life. The key is to come to a nagomi with the particular circumstances you happen to be born into.

We know there is no such thing as a perfect life but, too often, people think there is a magical solution that will solve all their problems. As we all know, money can't buy happiness, let alone love, but we sometimes might think that it can. Or you might believe going to a college with a good reputation is the be-all and end-all, but even if one could do that, it wouldn't necessarily mean that all life's problems would be automatically solved. One educator based in Japan once told me her experience of meeting with some Harvard student assistant staff. She was told that even after they had graduated from Harvard, landed lucrative jobs, and raised families in huge houses, some graduates still felt desolate and unhappy. There are similar stories in Japan; individuals who have graduated from the nation's top universities, such as Tokyo, Kyoto, Keio, or Waseda, do not necessarily have a satisfactory life.

Here, two metaphors might be handy to put things in perspective: the silver bullet and the magic carpet. The silver bullet refers to the idea that there is somehow a perfect solution, a key ingredient that could solve all our problems. On the other hand, in the magic carpet metaphor there are many different aspects that make your life good. Combining these aspects, rather than relying on just one thing to improve your life, is the path to achieving life satisfaction.

In general, there is no silver bullet that can kill the beast and magically solve all your problems, but people tend to waste too much time looking in the wrong places for this kind of answer. Searching for the silver bullet is one of the most disruptive fallacies in life. You might find a silver lining, but probably never a silver bullet.

It's much better to look to a combination of many elements—such as your relationships, your work, and your lifestyle—to help you to feel happier. This is the magic carpet solution, in which various different factors help you to float over the sea of desolation and disaster. This is the solution that can lead to better nagomi, both with yourself and with your environment. It is not a fight-or-flight situation, where we run away from things that make us unhappy or wish we just had a different job or family, or more money. It is a stay-and-nagomi opportunity.

Self-esteem is an important part of achieving nagomi. Self-confidence is a good thing so long as it does not go too far, as too much of it will result in an unbalanced life. If your ego is too big, you can lack the compassion and humility to be a good friend or partner. You can overlook the quieter people and arrogantly assume you know best when you might benefit from listening to others, even if they are not as outwardly confident as you may be. The nagomi of self-esteem is knowing your true self, your good and your bad points, and accepting them. Embracing the things you cannot change is a fundamental aspect of the nagomi of the self. One way to apply this to your life is to forgive others, rather than hold on to anger or resentment or guilt. You have to forgive yourself for past transgressions and similarly forgive others for things they have done against you. You can't achieve nagomi if you don't have this balance.

If you accept who you are, nobody can make you feel bad about yourself. What other people say or do cannot affect you, because self-esteem gives you the ultimate resilience. An Australian friend of mine, who is now based in Tokyo, once quipped: "There will always be people who are smarter than you, richer than you, and better looking than you. But remember, there is nobody better at being you than you!"

Another of the crucial ways to arrive at a nagomi of the self is *gaman*, which is a Japanese concept related to perseverance. It is one of the most important premises of Zen Buddhism and its principles have long been widely glorified and practiced, especially among the samurai class in the Middle Ages. You may think that, since the samurai warriors were the ruling class, they would have had their own way in life, and that their values wouldn't be particularly relevant to us in the modern day, but gaman, or self-restraint, could well be the ethics of the twenty-first century. For example, if you were on a spaceship, gaman could be one of the best virtues that you could have. A trip to Mars would take months. During that time, practicing self-restraint, gaman, especially in the context of not bothering other people and not requiring too much of the limited resources on board, would be essential. In fact, the selection process of astronauts already focuses on candidates' capacity for self-restraint.

However, no matter how we may work to improve the conditions around us, it is not possible to make a perfect world; indeed, the very premise of a perfect world has repeatedly led to earthly conditions of dystopia. With a bit of gaman, we may be able instead to achieve a nagomi with the imperfect world we live in.

So, the nagomi of self is contingent upon attaining self-knowledge, acceptance, forgiveness, and self-esteem. In its most extreme and simple form, the nagomi of self would lead to the erasing of all traces of ego-centered concerns. In Japan's youth culture, as we have seen in the cases of Yutabon and Higashide, there is a unique approach to the establishment and maintenance of the self within the social context, with elements also of release from the self. And there is always a sense of Zen meditation, even at the height of one's social media hype. In Zen Buddhism, the essential wisdom is about being released from your worldly desires and establishing a balance within yourself undisturbed by what happens outside. Meditation helps you develop the mindfulness to achieve all this. It is as if one could be a Zen priest in the sea of paparazzi and comment-hungry reporters. The key to understanding the Zen of social self in Japan is anonymity.

To a passing observer, Hiroyuki Nishimura, dressed casually with a signature beard on his chin, would seem like a typical guy, but he is the founder of Japan's 2chan, which was at one time the world's largest anonymous bulletin board, and he now owns 4chan. (Incidentally, it's sometimes pointed out that Hiroyuki looks like the popular depiction of Guy Fawkes in the masks worn by people involved in the Anonymous movement. I personally agree.) People use these bulletin boards to talk with other anonymous users about topics ranging from shared interests, such as anime and manga, to more serious discussions about politics, identity, and mental health. The fact that everyone is anonymous on these sites means that they can be more forthright with their views and less concerned about being judged. This is mostly a good thing, although it can facilitate darker activities including cyberbullying and threats of violence. I have met Hiroyuki many times, and he is a nonchalant, unassuming person who comments on many public affairs, but is almost never focused on promoting his own self-interests. He is not someone who would push himself up to the front for his own benefit, as many "influencers" on the internet are wont to do.

Hiroyuki's attitude is characteristic of Japan's internet culture, where a spirit of anonymity and ethos of "it's not about me" rule. A significant majority of Twitter accounts in Japan are anonymous, perhaps because many people feel that they are able to express their opinions more freely in this way. Although this predominance of anonymity has its own downsides and problems in terms of promoting public discourse, the "it's not about me" ethos has helped to generate many interesting internet memes, including emoji, which is now an aspect of online culture we can't imagine ever not existing. Emojis could not have arisen if it were not for the general tendencies of the Japanese to hide behind memes, instead of coming out of the comfort of anonymity to express themselves. Emoji is the result of a nagomi between the urge to express oneself and the need to remain anonymous. The same is true in the world of anime. For many years in the past, the voice actors (*seiyu*) in Japan whose voices featured in anime works remained for the most part anonymous, except to the most avid and inquisitive fans. Certainly, some voice actors who feature in major anime works are known both by their name and their face, but it is generally accurate to say that the world of Japanese anime has remained wonderfully anonymous, with many seiyu recognized by their voice alone, and not by their names or faces. This is a good example of the Japanese approach to individuality: to have a nagomi with anonymity while expressing, in another way, one's individuality in full bloom.

The latest phenomenon in Japan is "vocalo-p," or vocaloid producers. A vocaloid is a singing voice synthesizer that was pioneered by Yamaha in 2004, and it has recently become a platform for young composers to release their music. Waves of vocalo-ps have successfully published their music, sung by the vocaloid artificial intelligence, and a significant majority of vocalo-ps have remained anonymous, having never released their names or pictures of themselves. Some of these videos boast millions of views and their creators are making a lot of money. Indeed, it can be said that anonymity is one of the most remarkable trends in Japan's creative industry today.

In Japan, anonymity has always been a big part in the construction of the self in the social context. In Japan's *waka* poetry tradition, it is acceptable and often even fashionable to submit and present a work as *yomihitoshirazu* (literally, "author unknown"). Sometimes, emperors and other nobles would craft a *waka* poem and sign it as being by "author unknown," due to the sensitivity of the subject or the particular social situations involved. Many of them are romantic love poems, involving passionate emotions and wild imaginations. A yomihitoshirazu waka poem from the tenth century wishes that the cherry blossoms would fall heavily, so that the road would become invisible, preventing a lover from going away. A yomihitoshirazu waka poem would then often find its way into a prestigious collection of poems, edited by the royal court and endorsed by the emperor.

Most significantly, Japan's national anthem, *Kimigayo* ("Forever your reign"), has lyrics that date back to the *Kokin Wakashū* (*Collection of Japanese Poems of Ancient and Modern Times*), which was published around the year 905, and was written by a yomihitoshirazu. In Japan, anonymity has always been a socially accepted attitude. It is a respectable mode in which to express oneself, even to the degree that a poem by an unknown author could become the lyrics of the national anthem.

Here are the lyrics in full (it is one of the world's shortest national anthems):

Kimigayo wa
Chiyo ni yachiyo ni
Sazare-ishi no
Iwao to narite
Koke no musu made

Thousands of years of happy reign be thine;
Rule on, my lord, until what are pebbles now
By ages united to mighty rocks shall grow
Whose venerable sides the moss doth line.

The English translation is by the British Japanologist Basil Chamberlain. The culture of anonymity runs deep in the land of the rising sun, and the ethos of anonymity as an expression of individual existence has deep resonance with Japan's culture of nagomi. Anonymity is a beautiful example of the nagomi of the self in society, where the fruits of creativity are not necessarily associated with individual identities.

Anonymity is also the thread that ties the world of the gods together. In Japan, it is believed that there are eight million gods (*yaoyorozu no kami*); eight million is a metaphorical number that represents infinity. So, a god or goddess attains an almost anonymous status in the theology of Japan, not because He or She is insignificant, but because a god or goddess, no matter how important He or She may be, is just a drop in the vast ocean of gods supposedly reigning over this Earth. A Shinto shrine in Tokyo or elsewhere might proclaim that it is enshrining this specific god or goddess, but from the worldview of traditional Shinto, the particular name of the deity enshrined there does not need to be crucially important when people pay respect at the shrine. It is as if the worshipper is bowing before a collective concept of gods, or indeed a nagomi of the eight million (infinite) gods. In Japan, for culturally specific reasons, creators of culture such as manga, anime, games, and music are often called gods, but this naming does not invoke serious theological connotations. There is a clear continuum of mindset where the realm of gods is strongly linked to the world of creators, and where an important unifying thread is anonymity.

The relative unimportance of the individual in social life, especially in the creative process, is an interesting aspect of the Japanese culture. You may think that disregarding the role of each person might lead to a deterioration of the quality of works produced, but quite the opposite seems to happen. When one is not hindered by the importance of the self, one is released from its many and various limitations, maximizing the exercise of creative power. Some people are disapproving of the practice of anonymity in Japan; indeed, 2chan has been heavily criticized and has even been the subject of several lawsuits. However, even out of this—what some describe as a "hotbed for social evil"—has flourished some wonderful flowers of creativity, essentially through the power of anonymity.

Some people might prefer a way in which one expresses their unique identity freely and takes all the credit for it. Others might say that being anonymous is a second-class way of living, compared to a path of the more glamorous celebrity culture more common in the West. That may be so. However, the way the vocal-ops, voice actors, and the anonymous person who crafted Japan's national anthem found a nagomi between the self and society, through the shelter of anonymity if necessary, should be an inspiration for at least some of us. It does make the spectrum of the possible dynamics of establishing the self in society much broader.

Most importantly, if you are an introvert, by applying these techniques of social nagomi you can achieve great success while remaining private, staying distant and aloof, like the moon in the sky.

The nagomi of self allows the expression of your unique identity within the context of society. In a society often dominated by influencers and echo chambers, the nagomi of self enables a sustainable and creative way of allowing the self to be robustly connected to the society in general, while maintaining some healthy distance.

CHAPTER 4

Nagomi of Relationships

It's safe to say that emotions play an important role in our lives and relationships. Without emotions, it would be difficult to communicate effectively with people, but an unrestrained release of emotions can lead to conflict, both big and small. In order to achieve nagomi in relationships, it is important to be emotionally balanced, and in this regard, Japanese people have a distinctive set of life hacks.

The ethos of nagomi in the context of relationships is that maintaining harmony is the single most important thing, even if it masks differences of opinion below the surface. Nagomi is the idea that you would be best advised to avoid decisive confrontation at all costs. You can have a lively conversation and even disagree, but you should never break ties. It does not make sense to be selfish and create rifts. This may seem to be anathema to the Western love of heated discussion and debate, but in the context of today's polarized political landscape, there is something to be said for the ancient art of Japanese harmony, nagomi.

At the heart of nagomi is the idea that the relationship itself is the most important thing. Individuals all have value and are essential, but each person is defined first and foremost by their relationships; and disagreements and differences of opinion can be negotiated, or even ignored, in order to maintain a relationship. This principle is most useful when it comes to the relationships we don't choose, such as family and, to some extent, coworkers.

The Japanese approach to maintaining nagomi in relationships, coupled with the perceived inconspicuousness of the Japanese character, might seem on the surface to be the antithesis of the freedom of expression and development of individuality. However, it is indeed possible to have the freedom for both self-expression and nagomi. In order to understand the very creative way that the Japanese achieve this combination of a nagomi of relationships between the self, others, and the environment, let's consider the art of gardening.

In the Japanese gardening tradition, *shakkei* (borrowed scenery) is a way to establish nagomi between what you have designed of your own creation and the world at large. By applying *shakkei*, you achieve a balance between the garden you create and what was already there from the beginning. You cannot change the natural landscape, such as rivers and mountains, and that is why many famous gardens are built on the principle of shakkei. For example, the Genkyuen Garden in the city of Hikone is borrowing the views of the adjacent Hikone Castle, a samurai-period masterpiece designated as a National Treasure. In Kyoto, the Katsura Imperial Villa is famous for its shakkei principle. If you are lucky enough to visit Katsura, you will be thrilled by the sheer beauty and elegance of its buildings and landscape, which ingeniously incorporates its surroundings.

I believe the most dramatic shakkei garden in Japan is the Sengan-en house and gardens in Kagoshima, southern Japan, where the modernization of Japan started. A UNESCO World Heritage registered site, Sengan-en embraces the entire Kinko-wan Bay and the active volcanic island Sakurajima as shakkei. When you walk in the Sengan-en gardens, it's as though the grand mountain and ocean views are integral parts of the garden-scape. The trees, rocks, and waters within the gardens are designed in such a way that they look best when viewed against the backdrop of the existing world outside. This is a tour de force of creativity and nagomi, and it inspires people in Japan and the wider world to this day.

In a Japanese garden, the ideal is to strike a nagomi between the artificial and the natural so that there is a continuum of what you build intentionally and what was there from the beginning. This philosophy extends to how in Japan we try to go about conducting and nurturing our relationships.

You shouldn't try to change the people around you. You should let them be and instead focus on becoming a unique individual yourself. Through shakkei, you may even be a better person when you are juxtaposed with other people. Indeed, the individuality of a person can often shine more when flanked by other people. That is why couples call each other their "better half." Interestingly, it appears that a person is better at expressing their own identity in a creative way when nagomi of relationship is achieved.

In Japanese, *en* can be roughly translated as "relationship" and can also specifically refer to fate, luck, or chance. When you are in en, it means that your relationship with someone reflects the whole network of connections that exists in the world. When a relationship is successful, its success is often attributed to en, rather than individual merits or effort. En is a crucial concept in the understanding of how to achieve nagomi in relationships.

The importance of the nagomi of relationships becomes particularly evident in the face of conflict. It is considered very important to keep the en alive despite inevitable differences in opinions and values, and to keep making a sustainable nagomi of relationships.

In Japan, there is an entire genre of art dedicated to the idea of keeping the nagomi in relationships. The traditional art of *rakugo* is a wonderful example of the application of the spirit of nagomi, particularly in confrontational situations. Indeed, the laughter in rakugo is perhaps as close as you can get to the way of nagomi in comedy, at least in the context of Japanese tradition. Laughter is a successful method of keeping the nagomi of relationships, as it improves the ability to see oneself from the outside.

In rakugo, a single storyteller assumes the role of different characters, often in stories involving conflicts. For example, a single rakugo artist would portray both the wife and husband in a heated domestic dialogue. In one famous rakugo piece known as *Shibahama* ("Shiba Beach"), there is a series of lively conversations between a fishmonger and his wife living in the Tokyo of the pre-modern era. It is a genre of rakugo called Ninjo Banashi (Heartfelt Tales), which are stories that are humorous but ultimately quite moving.

What follows is my own translation, based on my memory of listening to Shibahama countless times from my childhood. Depending on the rakugo artist, the details of the story and character depictions can vary. So, what you read here is a generic retelling constructed from my own memory. It's a masterpiece of rakugo, as well as a beautiful embodiment of the nagomi of relationship.

This is how it goes. The protagonist, Kumagoro, had been a skilled craftsman with many loyal and admiring customers who enjoyed the good quality fish he brought to their doors. However, he develops a fondness for sake (given the excellent quality of Japanese sake, who doesn't?) and drinks far too much. Fishmongers need to go to the market early in the morning to purchase fish and prepare it for their customers, but because of his heavy drinking, Kumagoro cannot get up early in the morning and arrives at the market late, when the top-quality fish is all already gone. Kumagoro's customers, being connoisseurs with a keen sense of what is good, notice this, and gradually shy away from purchasing his fish. Kumagoro of course realizes what is happening, but out of wounded pride he pretends not to care. Thus begins the vicious circle: Kumagoro drinks more and more heavily, until he can no longer get up in the morning and no longer goes to the fish market at all.

One morning, after Kumagoro has drunk a lot of sake the night before, his wife awakens him and tells him that it is time to go to the fish market. Pushed by

his insistent wife, Kumagoro gets there before dawn and goes to the oceanfront to refresh his mind. As the sun rises, he notices something on the shore, and when he picks it up, he realizes it is a wallet. He takes the wallet back home, and when he opens it, he discovers there are fifty ryo of gold coins (roughly equivalent to fifty thousand US dollars today) in it. Overjoyed, Kumagoro goes on a spending spree. Being a fundamentally good-natured fellow, Kumagoro orders bottles of sake with expensive tsumami such as sashimi and sushi, invites his friends over, and starts a big banquet. After much eating, drinking, and merriment, Kumagoro, intoxicated again, goes to sleep.

When Kumagoro wakes up, his wife urges him to go to the fish market and start the work of the day. Kumagoro laughs and says that he doesn't have to work anymore, since he has gotten lucky with the wallet. The wife shakes her head and says she doesn't know what Kumagoro is talking about. He must be dreaming, she says. There was no wallet, and the previous day he had gone on a spending spree without having a way to pay for it all and is now in debt. Kumagoro cannot believe his ears. He is sure he found the wallet, but as he talks with his wife, he becomes less and less sure, realizing that his memory is fuzzy as to what happened. Finally, Kumagoro admits that it might have been a dream. He is shocked he has been drinking so much that he is this delusional. Kumagoro vows never to drink sake again, then goes to the fish market.

From that day on, Kumagoro works diligently. Because he has an eye for good fish and the skills to prepare it expertly, his customers return with a vengeance.

Kumagoro's popularity explodes, and he earns a lot of money.

A few years later, Kumagoro and his wife celebrate New Year's Eve. They have saved so much money that they now have their own store on the main street. They enjoy an incredibly affluent life, unthinkable just a short while ago. Kumagoro's wife thanks him for his hard work and says that there is something she needs to tell him.

"Do you remember the wallet that you found at the oceanfront near the fish market?"

"Yes, but I thought that was a dream."

"I told you it was a dream at the time, because I was afraid of the consequences. After you went to sleep, I asked the wise old man in town for his advice. He told me that it was wrong to keep the money. We should take it to the officials, he said. I thought that was the honest thing to do. So, when you woke up, I told you it was a dream. You believed me, like a good man, and started to work diligently. After a while, since nobody made a claim on the wallet and money, the officials gave them back to us. So, the wallet and money are here, and they are officially yours. I am very sorry to have told you a lie."

Kumagoro is amazed as he learns that what he was told by his wife at that time was a lie, and his "dream" was actually something that really happened.

"Are you angry with me?" asks his wife timidly. Kumagoro smiles.

"No, dear, I am not angry. Because of your wit and plan, I came to my senses and rediscovered the value of honest work. If I had spent the money, I would have been found out and caught by the officials. I would have been punished. You saved me. I thank you for that."

Kumagoro's wife weeps with joy. They are so happy together.

"Would you like to have some sake?"

"But I have stopped drinking."

"It is quite all right. This is New Year's Eve. We deserve to celebrate."

"But there is no sake in our house."

"Leave it to me. I have prepared everything."

Kumagoro's wife brings sake, kept at the optimum temperature.

"Is that so?" Kumagoro beams. Overjoyed, he holds the cup of sake up to his nose. "Hello, my old friend, long time no see. You smell so good. Ah, sake is so nice, isn't it?"

As Kumagoro is about to take the first sip, he abruptly stops.

"What is wrong?" his wife asks him.

"I will not drink."

"Why?"

"It might turn out to be a dream again."

With that wonderful punchline, the rakugo master takes a bow and leaves the stage, having delivered one of the best-known and most cherished routines in rakugo.

The way a rakugo piece is written and delivered is interesting from the point of view of nagomi. The format of a single player playing all the characters nurtures a sense of nagomi of relationships, as the player and the listeners must take on the viewpoints of often opposing agents in turn. In a lengthy piece with elaborate storylines, it is possible for a rakugo artist to be more than ten different characters. In the case of Shibahama, with a single rakugo artist portraying the fishmonger Kumagoro and his wife, the very fact that a single person can portray the voices of two characters with these antagonistic opinions is a wonderful example of the spirit of nagomi.

This represents the way we try to establish nagomi in Japanese society, no matter how antagonistic other people's opinions might be. There is something deeply moving about the rakugo approach, where the resolution usually depicts a position of harmony between the characters.

Rakugo also shows one essential element of how Japanese people achieve a nagomi of relationships: *zatsudan*.

Zatsudan is a Japanese word for describing small talk. *Zatsu* refers to the rich diversity of topics within a conversation and *dan* has to do with the colorful narratives that are captured in people's idiosyncratic conversations. Zatsudan captures the diverse and often unpredictable conversations that people engage in while drinking tea, having dinner, or just standing together on the street. Zatsudan is the essential spirit of the nagomi of conversation, and it plays an important role in communication. Indeed, the art of rakugo is thought to have evolved from zatsudan; in the samurai-ruled Edo era of Japan (1600–1868), performers are said to have given entertaining zatsudan in front of rich merchant patrons.

Zatsudan is spontaneous and creative, and rakugo is a wonderful example of it in action. In Tokyo's music halls, it is customary for the performer to adjust and fine-tune details of the act according to the audience present in the theater on that day. That is why there are several versions of such classic masterpieces as Shibahama. There is even a tradition of *Sandaibanashi* ("Three Themes Story"), where a skilled performer creates an entirely new rakugo story on the spot, based on three different themes proposed by randomly chosen members of the audience. Shibahama was created by the legendary rakugo master Sanyutei Encho in the nineteenth century, and he based it on the themes of "drunkard," "wallet," and "Shibahama" that were supplied by members of the theater audience.

There is something sublime and even noble in the concept of "zatsu," the adjective in the word *zatsudan*.

The word *zatsu* can be translated as "miscellaneous," "wild," or "diverse," and it is used in many different contexts. For example, the Japanese word for magazines is *zatsushi*, the word for miscellaneous plants is *zatsuso*, and a dog or cat of mixed breed is *zatsushu*. "Zatsu" represents the breadth and depth of things we encounter in life, and it is thus a celebration of diversity.

On the other hand, zatsu can sometimes have negative connotations. Japanese people also love the antithetical concept of purity, and the word *ma* refers to the idealized concept of purity, as in *mashiro* (pure white), *maatrashii* (pure new), and *magokoro* (pure heart). The nagomi of relationships can only be achieved when you successfully strike a balance between the zatsu (miscellaneous) and ma (pure). In the Japanese philosophy of life, it is generally considered that we need both the pure and the miscellaneous to sustain life. As we discussed in chapter 2, in order to enjoy and benefit from food through the practice of kounaichoumi (cooking in the mouth), we need both rice (which is pure) and okazu (which is miscellaneous) to support a healthy and robust life. In an izakaya, it is the combination of sake (which is made from rice, and therefore pure) and tsumami (which is miscellaneous) that makes the culinary experience so enjoyable.

Nagomi is all about finding a balance in all relationships. This can be particularly difficult to achieve in romantic love, which can disrupt the most measured of minds. There is something fundamentally unsustainable in romantic love. Romeo and Juliet's very romantic love thrives for just four days; it is anybody's guess how their love would have evolved had it lasted longer. One can only hope that, given more time, they would have discovered the nagomi of love.

This is exemplified beautifully in a film by the Japanese director Yasujiro Ozu, who I will speak about in more detail in chapter 6. One of his less well-known films, *Ochazuke no aji* ("The Flavor of Green Tea over Rice"), demonstrates nagomi in the context of romantic love. In the film, a husband and wife go through a kind of midlife crisis, with the wife (played by Michiyo Kogure) thinking that her husband (played by Shin Saburi) is too dull to be the subject of her ardent love. The seeming staleness in their domestic relationship changes when the husband is ordered by his company to go to Uruguay alone. The wife does not think this abrupt departure of her spouse is important enough for her to go to the airport to see him off. However, in his absence she realizes just how important he is to her. When he returns home unexpectedly, saying that there was trouble with the plane, she is overjoyed. The film ends as they go into the kitchen to make a bowl of *ochazuke* (a simple dish made by pouring green tea over a bowl of rice) together. It is not a very romantic meal—no candles, no glasses of champagne, nor white linen on the table—but their subdued love for one another is clear and it makes for a very moving film.

I wonder if a treatment like this would have made sense outside of Japan, where romantic love rules. For a typical Japanese audience, the seemingly mundane ending of *Ochazuke no aji* would have made much sense, at least when the film was released (1952), when arranged marriages, the very antithesis of romantic love, were still quite common within Japanese society. Perhaps even today, Japanese love is best symbolized by the act of sharing a bowl of rice with tea poured over it. It is consistent with the way of the nagomi of life to embrace the evolution of a relationship; it would not do to try to stay in the same state of heart as in the initial romantic love days. Life is about change, and it is beautiful to grow together.

CHAPTER 5

Nagomi of Health

Japanese people are said to have the longest and healthiest lives of anyone in the world. The idea that there is something special about Japan that promotes a long and healthy life has been around since ancient times.

In a Chinese legend, the alchemist and explorer Xu Fu was sent by the emperor Qin Shi Huang to the east sea in search of the elixir of life. Qin Shi Huang was the first emperor of unified China, founding the Qin dynasty. Although Qin Shi Huang was very powerful, without a parallel on this Earth, his only fear was the inevitability of death. Qin Shi Huang therefore sent the famed Xu Fu to the legendary Mount Penglai, where the elixir of life, which would give the drinker eternal life, would be found.

Unfortunately for Qin Shi Huang, Xu Fu never returned from his trip to the east sea. Legend has it that Xu Fu did reach a place called Mount Penglai, and having found a paradise, chose to live there by himself, rather than to report back to the anxiously waiting emperor.

While I'm yet to discover the elixir of life for myself, it's true to say that Japan is a country where the secret recipe for longevity seems to reside. This secret does not depend on one magic potion, but rather is the result of a holistic attitude toward life; and at the center of it all, you will find nagomi.

Nagomi is at the heart of the health of Japanese people. Of course, improvements in living conditions and advancements brought about by science and technology have increased life expectancy in many countries. In addition to these advantages is the nagomi of health, which is a realization that well-being depends on many different elements and that striking a balance between these elements is crucial for the maintenance of good health.

In general, when there is a problem in life we tend to focus on a single factor, because it is conceptually easy to do so. For example, we might take vitamin D pills instead of walking outside, an activity the Japanese call *shinrin-yoku* (forest bathing), and basking in the natural light, even though the latter approach would work in better and more sustainable ways.

I mentioned the difference between the silver bullet and the magic carpet approaches earlier, and the nagomi of health should be based on the magic carpet approach, rather than the silver bullet approach. Besides balancing different factors in your life, another important element of nagomi of health is to face your own desires. I wrote about *ikigai* (finding joy in everything you do) in my last book, and this concept is closely related to the nagomi of health.

In practical terms, there are many different aspects of ikigai. Even small things such as, for example, taking your dog for a walk or brewing a cup of tea in the morning could be your ikigai. On a more conceptual level, the essence of ikigai is to do with flexibility and inclusion in relation to the people around you and within yourself.

In order to appreciate and apply ikigai in your life, it is crucial to understand what ikigai is not. It is not an ideology with a specific list of what to do and what not to do. There is a widely circulated Venn diagram of iki-gai, with four overlapping circles representing "what you love," "what the world needs," "what you can be paid for," and "what you are good at." The diagram states that the intersection between "what you love" and "what the world needs" is mission, that between "what the world needs" and "what you can be paid for" is vocation, that between "what you can be paid for" and "what you are good at" is profession, and that between "what you are good at" and "what you love" is passion.

There are ambiguities and differences of opinion as to the origin of this diagram, but it is certainly not Japanese. Seen from a Japanese perspective, there is something counterintuitive about how ikigai is represented in that diagram. It is too narrow and restricted. Ikigai is defined as something that satisfies all four requirements, which is a really stringent condition. It would indeed be nice to possess all these values, but that is too good to be true. Needless to say, if you can have an ikigai that satisfies all these conditions, then great; but striving to fulfill all these requirements could become an obsession and deprive you of the freedom to live a flexible life and to have an ikigai in the first place.

Ikigai actually has nothing to do with a Venn diagram; it is more flexible and tolerant than that. You may love to make music, but you may not be good at it at all. That is perfectly fine, and you can still make it your ikigai. You may enjoy drawing as an unpaid hobby and that would be great, as long as you have fun. You may want to study something even if the world does not need it, and that would still be your perfect ikigai. You certainly need to love something in order to have an ikigai. All the other aspects are unessential details.

The Hungarian psychologist Mihaly Csikszentmihalyi studied "flow," a state of mind in which you are absorbed in something. When you are in the flow, you exhibit your maximum performance, enjoying what you are doing to the utmost. You forget the passage of time and become oblivious of your own self. When you are in the flow, you become one with what you are doing, which is an essential element of ikigai and the nagomi of health.

More practically speaking, our diet is one of the most important aspects of the nagomi-based life. One of the things that you notice when walking around the streets of Tokyo is that there are fewer overweight people than you might encounter in other countries—unless, of course, you go to the Ryogoku area in the eastern part of Tokyo, where many sumo stables are located. The sumo wrestlers put on weight for professional purposes, and the traditional way of preparing food for the sumo wrestlers—known as *chanko*—makes it possible for them to gain weight while still maintaining good health. The chanko way of cooking, centered around tasty soup made from vegetables, fish, and meat and flavored with soy or miso, is one of the unsung delights of Japanese cuisine. The surprising agility of the overweight sumo wrestlers is a testimony to the excellence of the Japanese way of cooking and eating.

Aside from sumo wrestlers, in Japan, there is a more general ethos that one does not eat or drink excessively. The Japanese have a concept called *harahachibu*, which literally means "stomach 80 percent." It is the idea that you should stop eating before you are really full; that is, when you are only 80 percent full. This is a sensible strategy to avoid overeating, as there is a delay between

the time when the food passes your lips to when it reaches your stomach and intestine and then finally circulates in your blood to give you the feeling that you have eaten enough. Eating with the ethos of harahachibu is, in a nutshell, establishing nagomi with your appetite, and it could be one of the most effective health habits that you can acquire in your life.

A truly wonderful example of *harahachibu* can be learned from Zen priests. Eiheiji temple in Fukui prefecture in the the Chūbu region of Honshū is one of the most venerable places in Japan to train as a Buddhist priest. I once had a series of very interesting conversations with Jikisai Minami, a Zen priest who trained there for more than ten years. He told me about the very rudimentary diet that a disciple enjoys (or endures, depending on your perspective) in the temple. It is based on the system of *ichiju issai*, which literally means "one soup, one okazu (dish)," plus rice. Although the portions are small and the ingredients are limited, these meals are the culmination of wisdom accumulated over many centuries, mostly passed on as unwritten customs, and support the mind and body of young priests going through arduous training schedules (typically rising at 3 AM in summer and at 4 AM in winter in order to meditate as the sun rises).

Eating is considered an important and essential part of Buddhist training. Indeed, consumption of food is a form of meditation for these young priests. They eat in silence, giving thanks for the food they receive. The priests eat everything, leaving no trace of food behind, so that when they finish, the tableware is so clean it can all be put away, as it is, into a cloth and used again for the next meal.

After graduating from Waseda University in Tokyo, Jikisai Minami spent more than a decade at Eiheiji temple, during which time he transformed from an intellectual at one of Japan's most prestigious universities into a practicing Buddhist priest. Jikisai told me that these traditional meals are so balanced in terms of nutrients and portions that once the young priests arrive at the temple to take up their training, they are very healthy. Their skin becomes youthful and glowing and their bodies are slim and agile. Indeed, the Eiheiji priests carry an air of elegance befitting the models on a catwalk in a Paris fashion show. Jikisai told me that once he started to train in Eiheiji, he became more popular with women (yes, in modern Japan, Buddhist priests do get married).

Not everyone can adapt to this very arduous approach to food and life at the Zen temple, however. One time, when I visited Eiheiji temple in a taxi, the driver told me that sometimes he would take young priests back to the nearest station. These are the ones who could not take it anymore and were escaping from the temple, going back into a world where they could eat whatever they liked and as much as they wanted. It is only human, the taxi driver told me, laughing in a pleasant manner.

It's true that we can't all be Zen priests, but those of us in the secular world should still try to pay attention to our diet and make it balanced. The nagomi of health means it is important to have variety in what you eat. Indeed, it is interesting to observe that even a typical Japanese person who is not particularly health-conscious still tries to strike a balance in their diet; nowadays in Japan there is an increasing awareness of the need to eat a wide variety of food, to get to know the ingredients, nutrients, and cooking methods involved, as well as the environmental impact of food production. The word *shokuiku* (food education) is becoming popular among Japanese people.

Dr. Teiji Nakamura, a soft-spoken medical doctor who has dedicated his career to nutrition as a field of preventive medicine, celebrates the sophistication of the Japanese diet and believes it could serve as a model for people around the world who want to improve their diet. He has campaigned enthusiastically for the improvement of nutrition among the general public in order to maintain good health. Thanks to Dr. Nakamura and others like him, the school lunch menus provided in Japanese elementary schools are models of how to achieve a nagomi in diet.

Another benefit of the Japanese diet is its focus on nurturing good gut microbiomes. Fermented food, such as miso and shoyu, plays a significant role in Japanese cuisine. Originally, the fermentation technique was developed as a way to preserve food and drink before the technology of refrigeration was invented, and it is now understood to produce food that is very good for our digestive health and immunity. The process of fermentation produces microorganisms such as bacteria, yeast, and fungi, which convert the sugar and starch in the food into alcohols or acids that function as a natural preservative. Indeed, in most Japanese households, not a day goes by without miso and shoyu being eaten, and it is good news that the West is embracing fermented foods such as kombucha, kimchi, and kefir.

The consumption of foods and drinks that have undergone fermentation contains benefits to health

that stretch beyond food preservation. The transformation of sugars and starches enhances the natural, beneficial bacteria in food. These bacteria, known as probiotics or good bacteria, are thought to help a multitude of health issues, specifically digestive health.

Eating is a huge part of the nagomi of health, as is being active. The physical activities that the Buddhist monks engage themselves in are wide-ranging. The sweeping of the gardens and the cleaning of the temple floors are basic elements of the training. In extreme cases, a few elite monks would go on nightly marathons in the mountains—for as long as a thousand days—in an effort to attain enlightenment. From the modern perspective, these activities could be regarded as sports and games in the Buddhist tradition, nurturing the nagomi of health, which would eventually lead to enlightenment.

As well as obvious and formal ways of keeping fit and healthy, like sports and games as discussed above, shinrin-yoku, or forest bathing, can be regarded as one of the pinnacles of the nagomi of health.

The concept and practice of shinrin-yoku is becoming increasingly popular all over the world, and it is interesting to look at how it came into existence in the first place. Shinrin-yoku is a relatively new word, coined in 1982 by Tomohide Akiyama, the chief of the Ministry of Forestry at that time. *Shinrin* means forest, and *yoku* is a generic Japanese word used to describe bathing. As well as being used for talking about bathing in an *onsen* hot spring (*onsenyoku*) or ocean (*kaisuiyoku*), there is *nikkoyoku* (sunbeam bathing) and *getsukoyoku* (moonlight bathing). Akiyama

is originally from the area of Nagano. Nagano, which hosted the Winter Olympics in 1998, is located at the center of Japan, and is famous for beautiful mountain ranges and deep, pristine forests. Undoubtedly, Akiyama had an intimate experience of the forest as a child and a young man.

Immersing yourself in the environment of the forest is not unique to Japan. What is unique in the Japanese concept of shinrin-yoku is the idea that you bathe in the forest atmosphere. The Japanese ideal of bathing is to establish nagomi with the medium you are in, whether it is an onsen, the ocean, or the forest. If you are bathing in an onsen hot spring, you would try to establish nagomi with the hot, mineral-rich water by letting the heat activate several physiological reactions within your body, as well as absorbing the minerals through your skin. If you are forest bathing, you would try to establish nagomi with what surrounds you by immersing yourself through the five senses in the murmur of leaves, singing of the birds, and blowing of the wind. The beauty of nagomi obtained through bathing is that you can let yourself go, and allow your body and unconscious processes to do all the necessary work to achieve nagomi.

The essence of the concept of yoku is being one with something. Yoku can refer to immersing yourself in any ambient atmosphere. If you succeed at being one with the environment, that would be yoku. The concept of bathing, or becoming one with the environment and therefore achieving nagomi with oneself and the surroundings, is a very important part of Japanese values and ethos, perhaps at the very foundation of everything that is important in Japanese culture.

The fact that the concept of shinrin-yoku was originally proposed by the Ministry of Forestry chief suggests that Akiyama was seeking ways other than logging to support and justify the existence of Japan's forests. In order to keep the forest beautiful and thriving, human intervention is needed. The forest needs continuous human care and preservation. In an era when we increasingly need to seek a balance between human activities and the preservation of the environment, the direction that shinrin-yoku is pointing is an important and inspirational one.

Taking good care of your body and your mind is indispensable if you are going to achieve a nagomi of health. No single factor is enough to support us through the complexity of life. Exercise and rest, work and play, challenge and comfort, and success and failure all lead to a balanced and harmonious life. In the way we approach our health, we tend to focus on one element rather than the more complex whole; perhaps we should avoid oversimplifying the explanations for good health. Statements such as: "I go for a run every day and that's why I stay so healthy," "I eat a yogurt in the morning and that keeps me young," and "I smile whenever I meet someone, and that makes me happy" might sound reasonable enough but are likely to be misrepresentations of what is actually happening in terms of the nagomi of health. These may be good habits, but nagomi encompasses a whole spectrum of elements that contribute to our well-being.

You don't have to train as a Buddhist monk, but you can eat mindfully, be aware of how full you're getting, be thankful for the food you have received, and take advantage of fresh, seasonal, flavorful, and nutritious food. Trying to keep your room clean and neat can be a great exercise of nagomi, because it requires your full spectrum of attention and execution in a good balance. Spending time outdoors and really appreciating—bathing in—the atmosphere is important, whether you are actually forest bathing or appreciating the atmosphere of whichever place you choose.

By practicing all of these together and being mindful of the fact that there is no single silver bullet that will serve as the answer, you are well on your way to achieving the nagomi of health.

CHAPTER 6

Nagomi of Lifelong Learning

Throughout its history, Japan has never been a country of abundance. Even today, though Japan is very rich in terms of modern advanced technology, it has a scarce allowance of natural resources, such as oil, gas, and rare metals. The abundant natural resources are fresh water and seawater.

This is perhaps the reason why Japanese people have always been acutely aware that they had to rely on their brains to make a living. Ever since my childhood, I have often heard the adage from my parents and other grown-ups that "the brain is the only abundant resource in Japan."

Knowledge and wisdom are the natural reserves of the twenty-first century. In a sense, other people's experiences are a vast reserve of oil, to be tapped into by anybody at any time. However, for many of us, much of our education is squeezed into the early part of our lives and too often, the system of formal education makes learning feel like work, and graduation from school feels like an escape from the need to study. And yet life is long, and our capacity to learn and grow continues throughout our lives.

Lifelong learning is central to achieving nagomi in life, no matter how old you are. When we are young, we should always listen to older people, because we can benefit from their experience. Listening to elders is a motto often emphasized in Japanese culture. At the same time though, when we are mature, we should listen to young people, because they can tell us new things about which we are ignorant. We need both the wisdom of age and the new insights of youth to be a whole self.

Wisdom is paramount in Japanese culture. Yasujiro Ozu, arguably the greatest film director to have come out of Japan so far, was a master of nagomi. His films *Tokyo Story, Early Summer, Late Spring,* and *An Autumn Afternoon* all portray nagomi among people, especially in the family. His films are filled with acceptance of life's imperfections, and the inevitable changes brought about by the onward march of life, such as marriage and death. It would not be far from the truth to say that many Japanese people regard becoming the kind of character who features in Ozu's films, such as the understanding and all-accepting father, as the ultimate goal of lifelong learning. In the closing ceremony of the Tokyo Olympics 2020—held one year later than scheduled, in 2021, due to the coronavirus pandemic—the theme music of *Tokyo Story* was played as the Japanese national flag was brought into the stadium. The bittersweet music fitted the mood of the end of an Olympic Games held in difficult times. Ozu's masterpieces represent the highest appreciation of the preciousness and fragility of the nagomi of life, as they recognize the reality of human existence from a profound perspective.

Ozu's family came from Matsusaka, a small city in western Japan. Ozu spent his formative days as a boy in this city, and some suggest that the cultural atmosphere there deeply affected his later works. Matsusaka has produced another hugely important cultural figure in the history of Japan: Norinaga Motoori (1731–1801), arguably the greatest scholar of Japanology (in

Japanese, *kokugaku*, literally "national study") of the samurai period. Yasujiro Ozu is distantly related to Norinaga Motoori; Motoori was a part of the Ozu family, but abandoned the life of a merchant and changed his family name to Motoori, the traditional denomination on his father's side. It's quite fascinating that two of the greatest luminaries of Japanese culture came from the same small city.

In eighteenth-century Japan, the time when Motoori was active, there were no commercial publishers. He saved up his earnings, from working as a medical doctor for children, in a bamboo shoot, and when he had put aside enough money, he self-published his works, including a commentary on *The Tale of Genji* and his analysis of *Kojiki* ("Records of Ancient Matters"). Motoori's works are considered to have been epoch-making. Before him, nobody paid the same close attention to the *Kojiki* (composed in 711–712), although it was a valuable document on Japan's ancient history and mythology (which were often mixed, as they are in many other cultures). Motoori did everything for the sheer joy of learning and understanding. He was not paid for his work as a Japanology scholar; it was a labor of love.

Matsusaka was a city full of very wealthy merchants who enjoyed all the pleasures that this floating world can offer. When these merchants, who presumably had exhausted all the earthly joys and affluence that money could buy, came to Motoori's lectures, they discovered that learning about *The Tale of Genji* and *Kojiki* was much more pleasurable than material goods. It is so wonderful to observe how people can be transformed by learning, even by a very short exposure to a learning situation. In particular, meeting with someone who can inspire you, give you ideas and guidance for long-term goals, and leave a lasting impression on you would leave a great legacy in your life, even if that encounter only lasted for a short time.

Later in his career, Motoori wrote a short treatise on the learning process, *Uiyamabumi* (which literally means "First Steps into Mountains"), in which he likened a person's entry to the world of learning to the trainee Buddhist priest's initial journey to the mountains, where he or she would seek spiritual awakening.

Today, the Japanology school founded by Motoori continues to have a profound influence on how the Japanese people see themselves.

One of the most important insights of this story is that you can find nagomi from learning. The affluent merchants who flocked to Motoori's lectures could find nagomi with their otherwise materialistic way of living. This is a phenomenon we can observe even today, all over the world; many people who have struck it rich in, for example, the stocks trade cannot be satisfied by just being rich and searching for fulfillment in the culture and arts. They often buy, as one example, highly priced works of art. Some may say that this is a form of boasting about their riches, but deep down they are finding nagomi with their lives through the learning process facilitated by their exposure to culture and arts, not by the material possession of artworks alone.

About 150 years after Motoori's lifetime, his distant relative Yasujiro Ozu would shoot films revealing overarching human truths. When you watch Ozu's tranquil masterpieces, you see beautiful examples of the acceptance of life due to a long-term commitment to learning. They are wonderful statements of nagomi in the turmoil of postwar Japan, and they show us the great power of the learning process, especially as it is applied to truths of life that are dear to us.

To consider Ozu's maturity as a result of the nagomi of lifelong learning is inspirational. We can all attain wisdom for ourselves so long as we tap into one of the most important functions of the human brain: curiosity. Without curiosity, we cannot make new things. Curiosity is the way we are able to absorb a vast amount of information, integrate it with our own selves, and achieve embodied knowledge. We need curiosity to make our brain intellectually and spiritually hungry. In today's world, learning as a way to satisfy curiosity must be considered one of our basic human rights. It should therefore be endorsed at every level of society, at any age, in any culture.

For those who did not enjoy school, it is important to realize that learning is natural for the brain. Just as the heart keeps beating as long as we live, so the brain keeps learning. Learning is the air the human brain breathes.

In Japan, there has always been the idea that the object of learning was not just to absorb information, but also to become a better person. The Japanese word *do* (pronounced "doh") is the idea that by learning, you become a new and better you. The suffix "do" is attached to many disciplines to express this concept. For example, *judo* is literally the way of flexibility, *kendo* is the way of katana swords, *shodo* is the way of writing (calligraphy), *sado* is the way of tea, *kado* is the way of flower (arrangements), and *kodo* is the way of fragrances. When you learn judo, spirituality is considered very important. You don't just learn how to throw your opponent. In judo, the emphasis is on the mindset as well as on the physical movements of your body. You don't merely get stronger, but also grow spiritually. That's why, in learning judo, you pay a lot of respect to the *sensei* (teacher), who would teach you not only the techniques but also a whole philosophy of life. Likewise, ways to establish nagomi in your life could be a discipline in itself, perhaps called *nagomido* ("the way of nagomi"), although there is no such word in Japanese until now, as I write this.

Sodoku (simple reading) is the traditional way to start a robust learning curve that can continue for one's lifetime. In sodoku, one reads a venerable classic text aloud, typically imitating and following the reading of the sensei. It is important to realize that you don't necessarily have to understand the meaning of the words in order to start sodoku. The core idea of sodoku (not to be confused with *sudoku*, which is a logical puzzle involving numbers) is that what you read out loud is guaranteed to be a great resource for your lifelong learning, even if you don't understand it from the beginning.

Traditionally, Chinese classics such as *Analects of Confucius* and *Records of the Grand Historian* by Sima Qian, as well as Japanese classics such as *The Tale of Genji*, have been used as materials for sodoku. It is the core practice of sodoku to read the original text directly, not its interpretations or annotations. Thus, your mind is challenged to establish nagomi with the real thing from the very start.

Age is not important in sodoku. In learning sodoku-style, you completely ignore the grade system of schools. You tackle the most enigmatic and profound classic texts by reading them aloud, without necessarily understanding what it means, starting at the tender age of, say, five. This approach, which establishes a nagomi between the most profound texts and a (very) young mind, is perhaps Japan's best-kept secret to lifelong learning.

At its core, sodoku is a great way to stimulate and nurture our curiosity. As the brain is exposed to the brave new world of learning without any intervening contexts or explanations, curiosity explodes without limit. The curiosity spurred by sodoku is pure and intense. It is a wonderful and effective way to start a learning process that can last for the rest of your life.

The approach of sodoku can be applied in cultures other than Japan. Why not start reading in the sodoku style a world literature masterpiece that you always pretended to have read but have actually never turned a page of, such as *A la recherche du temps perdu* ("In Search of Lost Time") by Marcel Proust or *War and Peace* by Leo Tolstoy? Wherever you come from, there are works of literature that can kick-start your own version of lifelong learning. You could read in the sodoku style, for example, a Shakespeare play, or a novel by

Virginia Woolf or James Joyce. And you could have a child of five do the same. It doesn't really matter if the child does not have a clue about what he or she may be reading. It is simply crucial that the child has a feeling for what lies ahead, in the great challenge of learning that will continue throughout their life.

In the nagomi of lifelong learning as exemplified by sodoku, there are some important practical guidelines to be followed.

One, the emphasis is first and foremost on establishing familiarity with the subject. Whether it is a foreign language, mathematics, or programming skills, the nagomi approach to learning emphasizes the importance of time spent with the subject, in which one familiarizes oneself with what is to be learned even if one does not understand every detail from the beginning.

Two, a relaxed learning environment is necessary. Partly because many Japanese households tend to be small and have limited space, and partly because of the generally close ties between family members, it is not unusual for Japanese kids to study and do homework assignments in the living room, where their father might be drinking beer and watching television, their mother might be chatting on the phone, and their sibling might be playing Nintendo. Statistics show that those kids who study in the living room actually do better than those who study in their own rooms. Such a practice suggests the importance of a relaxed environment for learning, which is in harmony with the spirit of nagomi.

Three, in learning, one gradually tries to find nagomi with the subject one is studying at an ever-higher level. Indeed, achieving nagomi of familiarity with the subject is central to the Japanese approach to learning, an ethos to be found from craftsmen to the scientists at the frontiers of various fields.

You are never too old to be curious and try sodoku. After all, we know that lifelong learning is indispensable for our well-being and for keeping our spirit young, and it is our best hope of achieving nagomi with life's ups and downs. By continuously learning, we can embody a living wisdom in ourselves. Indeed, our lives are a constant learning process, and nagomi is the most valuable fruit of learning.

CHAPTER 7

Nagomi of Creativity

In 1945, a young medical student was taking a long walk through the city of Osaka, in the western part of Japan. At that time, almost the entire city had turned into a scorched flatland due to bombings by the United States Air Force. The young man was very hungry. He chanced upon a house that was still standing and knocked on the door. Opening the door, the residents of the house saw an earnest-looking young student in shabby clothes, bowing repeatedly, as if urged on by something. They felt pity and gave the student three generous pieces of onigiri (rice balls) out of their own scarce provisions. The young student ate them as if he hadn't touched food for a long time. On the strength of the onigiri and the kindness of those people, he walked the eleven miles (eighteen kilometers) from Osaka back to his home in the city of Takarazuka. He later learned that the house of the residents who so kindly gave him the onigiri was bombed a few days later.

It was during his long walk home that the young medical student made a resolution to become a manga artist. Nowadays, successful manga artists are highly regarded and well paid, but back when the student made his resolution, being a manga artist as an occupation was virtually nonexistent. Aspiring to this profession was like jumping into the ocean blindfolded. But as unpromising as his prospects must have appeared, if that young medical student had not made the decision to become a manga artist, the history of manga might have been quite different from what we know it to be today. It is fortunate for many of us that he went ahead with his fanciful ideas.

The name of the young medical student was Osamu Tezuka, and he became a prolific manga artist, known for such works as *Astro Boy*, *Princess Knight*, *Kimba the White Lion*, *Black Jack*, *Phoenix*, *Buddha*, and *Message to Adolf*. Tezuka was so creative and successful that he came to be known as the "Father of Manga" or even sometimes "God of Manga."

Tezuka's works had a huge impact on the general public and inspired many generations of manga artists. Not only that, Tezuka had a personal and warm hand in guiding aspiring young manga artists who flocked to him for teachings, inspiration, and mentorship, just as the merchants in Matsuzaka gathered around Norinaga Motoori for wisdom to guide them through life in this floating world.

We all need fiction to make living easier, better, and more tolerable. The harder the situation is, the purer and more profound the creative urge often becomes. It is anybody's guess why Tezuka resolved to be a manga artist on that particular day, and what the sight of his scorched homeland had to do with that resolution. But the emotional impact on young Tezuka does seem to have had a formative influence on his creative genius.

Manga is open to everyone to enjoy and create. As a schoolkid, I vividly remember writing works of manga (mine were mostly comedy, like the ones by Fujio Akatsuka) and comparing them with my friends'. Needless to say, they were of very low quality. However, the

assumption was that the art of manga could be tried by anyone, even if you had not received professional training.

This democratic approach to creativity has perhaps always been the hallmark of Japanese society. Especially when a field is young and active, there is not such a hierarchy of values. (In manga, there is no *New York Times*, *New Yorker*, or *Guardian* as gatekeepers of high values!) In Japan, there has never been such a sharp division between high and low cultures. There has always been a built-in nagomi between the cultural genres.

After modern Japan came into existence in 1867 with the return to direct rule by the emperor (which evolved later to a constitutional monarchy), the Tokyo government tried to incorporate the perceived high cultures of the West. As part of this effort, Japanese people started learning to paint in oils, write novels, perform and enjoy classical music, and stage Shakespeare plays in Japanese. There was a tendency, especially among those in power and those with an education, to make a distinction between high and low cultures, identifying the former with Western culture in general, and also with some traditional Japanese cultural forms such as kabuki, Noh, and bunraku puppet theater. In the eyes of the government, high cultural forms were particularly worthy of protection and promotion, as Japan tried to increase its prestige as a nation in the eyes of the Western nations. That was understandable in the historical context; Japan was playing a game of catch-up.

The beauty of manga is that there never was a sense of counterculture among the form's leading artists. The founding fathers of modern manga, although there was less public admiration for the genre than compared to today, did not much mind the lack of public respect. They couldn't have cared less. They did not have a grudge against those who practiced in cultural forms such as theatre or oil painting, and there was no sense of needing to rebel against perceived oppressors. Manga artists such as Osamu Tezuka and Fujio Akatsuka just went about their business of producing good work, and that was all that mattered to them.

In general, whenever something new springs up in the Japanese cultural scene, it happens in a relaxed way. It is as if nagomi is built into the very foundations of the Japanese psyche and new things spring up spontaneously, like bamboo shoots after the rain.

A sublime example, of course, is karaoke, which comes etymologically from "kara" (empty) and "oke" (a Japanese-style abbreviation for orchestra). Only in Japan, perhaps, would people have thought that amateurish singers would have their day by singing along with prerecorded musicians.

Being born and raised in Japan, I naturally come from a cultural background where you can sing before a lot of people without much regard for their quality assessments and the reception you might get. Karaoke in Japan is a far cry from the American hit drama series *Glee*, where a bunch of senior high school students exhibit almost perfect performance in singing and dancing. In Japan, people don't care whether you can sing well or not. The point is to have a good time (singing well may even put people off). There is no distinction between high (professional) and low (amateur), and if there was, it would be a continuum rather than a sharp division. Of course, karaoke is pretty popular in the West, too, and it's great that people around the world can enter a karaoke bar and have this kind of unselfconscious fun with their friends.

It has a lot to do with keeping your inner child alive. You can write manga, you can sing and dance, just like a carefree child, without caring too much what other people might think of you. It is an unfortunate fact that many people forget the simple joys of childhood creative activities. They become keenly aware of the possible criticisms that might be directed at their performance. As a consequence, they become coy and shy away from exhibiting their creativity. They would never dream of singing karaoke—a huge missed opportunity from the point of view of pursuing your creativity to the full. It is understandable, for sure, because humans are social animals and the ego must be protected. Such a psychological barrier can definitely be overcome by following the way of nagomi, which helps people remain young at heart even when they mature, keeping the inner child alive.

Nagomi is an important aspect of creativity for so many reasons. Key to the nagomi of creativity is an acceptance of youth and immaturity as a positive value.

Japan is a country that highly appreciates the value of remaining a child in spirit. One of the clues that shows you the high regard the Japanese have for anything kid-related is *kawaii*. This Japanese word, roughly equivalent to "cute" in English, is a very powerful wild card in the language when you want to make someone happy by praising them. You can, of course, say that a child is kawaii, or a cat is kawaii. That would be quite a conventional usage of the expression. In addition to that, though, you can say that a middle-aged man, or even an image of Buddha, is kawaii. Kawaii has a more universal applicability than its English counterpart "cute." Indeed, arguably the greatest Japanese novelist since Lady Murasaki, Soseki Natsume (1867-1916), was serious in his pursuit of a deep study of the human condition in modern society—and, at the same time, of kawaii. His debut novel, *I Am a Cat*, is regarded by many as both artistically deep and kawaii. The narrator is none other than a stray cat, who has been adopted into the house of a teacher, a clear reference to the novelist himself (Natsume taught at a high school and the University of Tokyo before becoming a full-time professional writer). The image of Natsume as a cat-lover is widely shared by members of the general public, and has helped make his works accessible, when they might otherwise have been regarded as too serious for a casual reader.

The association of kawaii with mature men is perhaps one of the best-kept secrets of Japanese culture; this is a country where even Arnold Schwarzenegger was considered to be kawaii at the height of his fame as the evil character in *The Terminator*. After he appeared in Japanese TV commercials, Schwarzenegger acquired the kawaii nickname "Schwa-chan" (chan is a ubiquitous suffix in the Japanese language that refers to infants or small children, or somebody equivalently cute.)

In a sense, kawaii is the uniquely Japanese way of blurring boundaries and establishing a nagomi between high and low cultures, male and female, the powerful and powerless, and the young and the old. Kawaii is a great equalizer of people. When someone is perceived to be kawaii, nagomi can be established, no matter what their gender, age, or social status might be. Kawaii belongs to the set of cognitive tools that one could employ to comprehensively embrace and include a wide diversity of people. With such a process, it is possible to express one's unique individuality without necessarily clashing with the status quo. That would actually be the true spirit of the nagomi of creativity.

Advancing freedom without disruption on the surface is a knack shared by many people in Japan. In a world where political correctness, cancel culture, and woke ways of thinking are sometimes perceived to be going too far (although, needless to say, the values and causes pushed forward in those movements can and should be endorsed), lessons from the nagomi of creativity might provide a spoonful of sugar to help the necessary transformations go down smoothly in society.

Whenever I think of the uniquely Japanese way of adapting to adversities, two examples pop up in my mind.

Both involve, in a nutshell, covert possessions of freedom as opposed to overt rebellion or assertion of liberty.

The first is the custom of *uramasari* (literally, "winning lining"), which flourished during the Edo samurai period. In those times, the ruling shogun would often declare a ban on luxury clothing materials as a means to curb an over-bullish economy or to impose an austere system of ethics (which was the belief that the ruling samurai ostensibly subscribed to). The townspeople of Edo (the ancient name for Tokyo) did not complain or demonstrate against this cultural oppression. Instead, they went about ordering specially designed clothes that were subdued on the surface but gorgeous inside, made from expensive materials such as silk or *kinran*, a special fabric woven from golden and silver threads. Thus, those with defiant spirits could wear what appeared to be a simple and modest fabric outside while secretly wearing a gorgeous lining, giving themselves a great morale boost and sense of pride without offending the ruling samurai. (The samurai most likely knew all about it, but just turned a blind eye.)

Another interesting example is the *matsuri* (festival) sushi that originates in Okayama, in western Japan. Here again, the ruling samurai class declared that in order to discourage a luxurious lifestyle, only one dish would be allowed at meals. The resilient townspeople of Okayama did not complain. Instead, they came up with the brilliant idea of matsuri sushi, which involved putting all the delicious ingredients available to them—such as fish sashimi, octopus, squid, shrimp, shredded egg, shiitake mushrooms, and *mamakari* (marinated scaled sardine, a specialty of Okayama)—in a wooden *oke* bucket, and putting vinegared rice over the top of it. As such, they were making just one dish, true to the order of the samurai lord; it just happened to have everything in it, and in addition they were hiding the ingredients with a tasty rice cover. Then, just before serving, they would turn the *oke* bucket upside down and place the matsuri sushi on a large plate, with all the juicy and colorful ingredients now visible on top of the vinegared sushi rice.

I regard these two examples as a particularly Japanese expression of the spirit of the nagomi of creativity. In each of these cases, people were securing their freedom while maintaining nagomi with the ruling class.

The epiphany that the young Osamu Tezuka experienced in the scorched flatland of postwar Osaka is a great example of the nagomi of creativity. He could have demonstrated in defiance of the atrocity of the war or the misjudgments of the government, but instead he went about making great works of manga that gave people much joy amid the difficulties of life in postwar Japan. That was Tezuka's nagomi of creativity.

When there is trouble, in addition to raising your voice directly against it, there might be alternative ways, less obvious or ostentatious but more effective, superficially shy but brave deep down. That is the way of nagomi or nagomido, in which one could be creative—in a big way—without being disruptive.

In the way of nagomi, the most important thing is being true to yourself.

People generally have the idea that a genius is a lone wolf or a maverick. There are certainly some examples of that. Albert Einstein, for one, who dropped out of Germany's strictly regulated gymnasium education system and wandered around Europe alone, was certainly a maverick. However, a genius must have nagomi with the times and the society, too, especially if they are to find some recognizable success. Genius needs to be conformist, even, in order to put one's potential in the optimum context so it might flower.

A crucial insight into the essential nature of genius is that nagomi is a process where more elements than one are merged to form a new entity. It is central to the Japanese understanding of what life entails, whether that be a life involving genius, a more mundane life, or anything else. The brain can be one big nagomi machine, where various neural circuits conducting different functionalities are merged, blended, and resonate with each other to give rise to new functionalities.

Within the Japanese psyche, genius is a part of life's great circle, rather than a gift coming from elsewhere. This is a completely different view of the creative process from that of the West.

In the Western cultural tradition, genius tends to be understood as something that stands alone. This image of genius may have its origin in the Biblical story of God creating the world (alone) in six days. Most definitely, the Western conceptualization of genius has nothing to do with nagomi, in which one establishes balance and harmony with the various elements that surround oneself.

In the Japanese tradition, nagomi is a delicate balance between self-assertion and self-negation, the absolute versus the relative values of being oneself. Creativity is not a process in which one's genius imposes itself on the world. Rather, it is a process of finding an organic blend between what is uniquely oneself and the broader aspects of the wider world. In this respect, nagomi is a truly creative process of finding an organic blend of the positive assertion of the self and the negation of the self, as one tries to find a coexisting solution with the world.

In sum, genius is a network phenomenon, in which one tries to establish a nagomi between one's own particular potential and the society one finds oneself in. Genius is the fruit of the nagomi of creativity.

Even when someone ostensibly creates something great, it is not considered attributable to the traits of the individual alone. The way of nagomi (nagomido) recognizes this, which opens up the possibility of creativity to everyone, no matter what their personal traits might be. If you know how to associate with the rest of the world in an appropriate way, then maybe you can accomplish something valuable. Such a line of thought might appear to be deflating for the ego, but it is actually deeply emancipating.

If your mind is set free from all presuppositions about creativity, such as ideas about high and low culture, talent, gender, age, and social status, then you have made the nagomi of creativity your own. I sincerely hope that the discussions in this chapter have helped you in waking up to the potential within you.

Maybe you will decide to book a karaoke night for your friends or colleagues, or to join a painting or drawing class even though you haven't painted or drawn since school. It is just a question of finding something that you love to do and will do without caring too much about what other people might think, as we all did when we were children and naturally creative.

When you have achieved nagomi with yourself and your environment and can smile in the cradle of your newly found secure base, breathing freely in a room of your own, you have prepared yourself to be creative to your fullest potential. You are on the verge of achieving a nagomi of creativity.

When you listen to your inner voice, no matter what the environment may be, you can always aim to exercise the way of nagomi in creative ways and overcome difficulties, both of society and of your own.

In the true spirit of the nagomi of creativity, you should always ask yourself: What will my verse be?

CHAPTER 8

Nagomi of Life

L ife is a journey, a one-way transition from youth to old age. Many of us struggle to accept this inevitability and perceive aging as something to guard against, as though it is a shameful defeat. But that is a misguided understanding of the essence of life. It is no exaggeration to say that applying nagomi to our lives will change the way we approach our own existence.

In a classic essay that has entered the canon of Japanese literature, *Hojoki* ("An Account of a Ten-Foot-Square Hut") by Kamo no Chomei (1155–1216), there is a wonderful passage about the transience of life. It begins with this famous opening sentence: "The flow of the river is always there, and yet, it is never the same water. The bubbles on the surface of water pools appear, and then disappear, in incessant changes."

Chomei is preoccupied by the passing of time and the contradiction between eternity and temporality.

He laments how people and houses flourish and then go without leaving a trace. He likens changes in places and people to the morning dew on an *asagao* (morning glory) flower. The dew cannot stay until the evening, Chomei writes. The flower itself would perish. Nothing is permanent, and that is the inevitable condition of life, he concludes dismally. Chomei wrote this pensive essay during his self-imposed retreat in a *hojo* (a ten-foot-square hut). Today, there is a reconstruction of his hojo in the Kawai Shrine in Kyoto, next to a beautiful forest.

It is fitting to start this chapter on the nagomi of life with Chomei's classic essay, as nagomi is the recognition of the fact that life depends on many elements for robustness, stability, and dependability. Without nagomi, life in this unpredictable world cannot go on. Nagomi is an important puzzle piece in the philosophy of life, not only in the Japanese context but in the wider world. Indeed, you may even say that nagomi is life itself.

If we look at the contemporary world and the things that seem big and important today, such as companies

like Meta, Alphabet, Apple, and Amazon, we might think they are too big to fail and struggle to imagine life without them. Yet they are far from permanent. For now, they appear to be invincible, and it's true that these companies are likely to stay with us for a few decades at least. However, if Chomei were alive today, he would predict great uncertainty. Because that's life.

The greatest tragedy of life often comes from resisting the changes that living our organic lives inevitably brings. Many cultures around the world are obsessed with youth, with people going to great lengths to stay young-looking, by trying this supplement or another, taking this exercise, eating that special food, and undergoing cosmetic surgery. These are all down to personal choice, but to endlessly pursue youth is to overlook the beauty that can come with age.

While Bob Dylan once sang about being forever young and is famed for a lot of his early music, he has continued to evolve as a musician and released a critically acclaimed new album, *Rough and Rowdy Ways*, in June 2020. I personally was stunned by the nature of this work, which is both mature and youthful at the same time. Dylan's voice sounds like an aged oak with a hint of honey, different from the trademark voice of his youth, but still deeply attractive.

The Japanese approach to staying forever young is not in rejecting change but embracing it as a natural occurrence in this floating world. In Japan, there is the concept of *tokowaka*, which literally translates as "forever young" ("toko" means eternity and "waka" means young). Tokowaka occupies an important position in the philosophy of life in Japan. Most significantly, tokowaka is a process; nothing stays the same and everything is renewed, just as Chomei observes at the beginning of *Hojoki*. Dylan coming up with the comeback single "Murder Most Foul" at the mature age of eighty is very tokowaka. In order to stay forever young, according to the philosophy of tokowaka, you need to let go, and embrace—even welcome—changes. Indeed, tokowaka is a process in which you establish a nagomi with aging.

The philosophy of tokowaka was celebrated by the founders of the Noh play, a Japanese theater tradition that is now on the UNESCO list of intangible cultural heritage. It was founded by Kan'ami (1333-1384) and Zeami (1363-1443), father and son, in the fourteenth century; integrates masks, costumes, and various props; and requires highly trained actors and musicians to enact. Kan'ami and Zeami also wrote a theoretical analysis of the stage titled *Fushikaden* ("Style and the Flower"), in which they distinguish between two kinds of "flowers," or the radiance of an actor on stage. One is "flower of the time," which is possessed by an actor in their youth. The other is "flower of the truth," appearing at a mature age, when they are wrinkled, slow in motion, and perhaps even bent. The "flower of the truth" is the forever young, or tokowaka, realized by the profound art of the Noh play through hard work and discipline.

One example of tokowaka in the natural world is the cherry blossom we see in the spring. The beautiful pink flowers of the cherry tree are indelibly associated with Japan and are celebrated for their ephemeral bloom. Everything about cherry blossoms is unpredictable. The time at which they bloom and the length of time they bloom for is determined by the fickle spring

weather; a number of warm days will bring the buds to bloom, subsequent cooler weather will preserve the blossoms for longer, but rain and wind can bring them prematurely to the ground. Even in the best conditions, the blossoms only last a week or so. For many Japanese people, cherry blossoms are a metaphor for life. Like our lives, their bloom is unpredictable and short, and at the whim of elements beyond their control. *Hanami*, "flower viewing," the Japanese tradition of the appreciation of flowers, is about enjoying life to the fullest while we can because one day it will end.

By repeating the natural process each year, the cherry blossom collectively achieves something akin to tokowaka, or the flower of the truth. It is a celebration of the ephemeral, or the flower of the time, according to Kan'ami and Zeami's work.

If you were to summarize the Japanese philosophy of life in one phrase, it would be that "the only permanence in this world is change." This is more obvious now than ever before with the COVID-19 pandemic. We have all been experiencing greater levels of uncertainty and have had to learn to cope with unexpected and uncontrollable changes. The way of nagomi recognizes that things can be complex and shows us that we have to be accommodating of ambiguity, uneasiness, and the other ups and downs that life can bring.

The sense of the ephemeral nature of the world, the realization that everything passes, is behind the Japanese embrace of nagomi. Everything passes, no matter how powerful and permanent it might appear to be. If you build something out of brick and stone, you cannot make it permanent. Even the rebuilding of the Ise Shrine every twenty years is just a best attempt at permanence in the face of the impermanence of nature.

Every twenty years, the shrine buildings are carefully dismantled and new buildings of exactly the same structure are erected on a new site, using newly obtained wood. The current buildings date from the year 2013. The next rebuilding will take place in the year 2033. Records suggest that this rebuilding process has been going on for the last 1,200 years, with occasional irregularities due to battles and social turmoil.

In order to sustain the exact rebuilding of the shrines every twenty years, a number of careful considerations and preparations must be put in place. For example, the *hinoki* (Japanese cypress) trees that are used as logs in the shrine buildings must be planted many decades in advance. For this purpose, the Ise Shrine has reserves of hinoki trees all over the nation. Some of the logs used for the shrine need to be of a certain size, which is only achievable by hinoki trees that are more than two hundred years old. The rebuilding of the shrine buildings over this long period of more than 1,200 years has thus

involved careful and extensive planning, and the nurturing of the Ise Shrine hinoki reserves.

And so, the Ise Shrine buildings are forever young, or tokowaka, even though materially speaking they are always changing. Indeed, the venerable shrine can stay young, new, and shining precisely because it is letting its older self go.

The Japanese approach to staying forever young, then, is not about rejecting change, but embracing it. Superficially, the Ise Shrine might appear to be about keeping up an appearance of being forever young by replacing the old with the new, thereby valuing only the latter. But it does not reject the notion that the new eventually becomes old; when the shrine is rebuilt every twenty years, the carefully dismantled wood from the old building, quite robust and strong still, is meticulously polished and processed, to be used for smaller shrines distributed around the Ise area. The wood is always respected and treated with great care, fitting for its venerable history of having once been used to build the Ise Shrine.

Even if the Ise Shrine stays forever young in a

superficial sense, then, we still accept that in this floating world, changes are natural. It may at first appear paradoxical that, despite being a nation built on an emphasis on the ephemerality of things and dedicated to the *mono no aware* ("pathos of things") in the floating world, Japan boasts some of the most ancient and long-lasting institutions in the world. The Kongo Gumi construction company was founded in 578 and still exists today. Japan is also the country with the oldest hereditary monarchy in the world, with the current emperor, Naruhito, being the 126th to sit on the Chrysanthemum Throne. It is as if the realization of the transience of life makes it possible to have a long-lasting format for business and monarchy. The key is embracing the way of nagomi in the face of inevitable changes in life.

Even if we can embrace the nagomi of life, we may still fear death, but we can establish nagomi with our own mortality by finding peace and harmony with loved ones who have passed away. In Japan, it is customary to have a special place within the home to commemorate the deceased. *Butsudans*, or Buddhist altars, are often found in Japanese households and are Japan's answer to how to find nagomi with the deceased, or death in general.

Butsudans are meticulously carved and polished and are typically surrounded with the memorabilia of the deceased by their loved ones, with items representing Buddhist beliefs. A *senko* incense stick is usually among the items, as it is believed that the smoke and fragrance provide food for the soul of the deceased. When people bring gifts such as sweets or fruits to the house, it is customary to put them first in the butsudan, as a symbol of offerings to the departed soul. Through these activities centered around the butsudan, you can keep talking to those loved ones who have passed away. The conventional wisdom is that people are never truly dead as long as you remember them. The butsudans function as a center of remembrance for loved ones, based on a set of practical routines.

In Shinto—the Japanese answer to Buddhism—people become gods after they pass away. It is not like the Western concept of a god who precedes and creates the entire universe. A god in Japan is more human. Indeed,

a god is nothing more than a deceased human, but they therefore have deeper and more intimate implications for our existence. A god is a form of nagomi with death.

When a person passes away, they may be recognized as a god and preserved in a Shinto shrine. The name given to the deceased as a god represents the perceived nature of the person in their life, in recognition of their personality, achievements, and favorite stories. The god-naming system is a practical way to establish nagomi with the deceased by keeping their memory alive.

Tokugawa Ieyasu, the samurai warrior who united Japan in the turmoil of the Sengoku period and laid the foundations for the Tokugawa Shogunate (1603–1868), was recognized as a deity with the name Tosho Daigongen (*tosho* means "east radiance," referring to the fact that Ieyasu chose Tokyo as the new capital, giving radiance to the eastern region of Japan; *Daigongen* is a honorary title). Sugawara no Michizane, an aristocrat in the Middle Ages (845–903), although an excellent scholar and poet, died in exile after a rivalry with the ruling clan at that time. After his death, he became Tenjin (literally "God of Heaven"), referring to the belief that his angry spirit started a thunderstorm in Kyoto (the capital of Japan at that time), causing a fire in which members of the clan who had expelled him perished. As years passed, Tenjin became the patron god of scholars, reflecting Michizane's excellent achievements during his lifetime. The name of a god in the Japanese tradition is something that is given in memory of a remarkable person who has lived their brief life on this Earth and then perished, as every one of us must do eventually.

Once, I had a truly revealing encounter with a young Shinto priest in Takachiho, in the southern part of Japan. Legend has it that the founding gods of Japan descended from heaven at Takachiho, so the mountainous location is considered to be the home of gods in Japan. While visiting this historically significant location, I exchanged some words with the Shinto priest, who was young and eager. The brief conversation inspired me as to the true essence of gods in Japan; it was truly an epiphany.

We were in front of the Amano Iwato (Heaven's Cave Door), where, in Japanese mythology, Goddess Amaterasu, the founding deity of all gods in Japan, hid during a time of misery in her life. Her brother Susanoo, being violent and wild, had been engaging in a series of atrocities, and Amaterasu could not take it anymore. She retreated into Heaven's Cave Door, and the whole world became dark, as if night had fallen. This can be taken metaphorically, although some scholars interpret it as a reference to a total solar eclipse in ancient times. Anyway, at the disappearance of Amaterasu, people were alarmed, as things were far from normal without her. Pressed to do something, they performed joyful music and dance in order to attract Amaterasu's attention. Intrigued by the festivities outside, Amaterasu opened Heaven's Cave Door ever so slightly. Then, people outside showed Amaterasu a mirror called Yata No Kagami (which is rumored to be one of the Three Sacred Treasures of the Imperial Household to this day, although nobody, including the emperor, has seen it). Enticed as she was by her own reflection in the mirror, there was a momentary lapse in Amaterasu's mind. The people took advantage of this, and gently escorted Amaterasu out of Heaven's Cave Door. The world became bright again.

A young Shinto priest was eagerly explaining all this to me and the other members of the public at the site that day. It was more of a touristy than a religious thing, but the priest, probably just out of Shinto school, was enthusiastic in his explanation.

Then, as if in passing, and apparently giving little thought to it, the young priest casually remarked: "So, that is the story of Goddess Amaterasu. When she was alive, she presumably had a name as a human, but we don't know what that was. It may have been Himiko (a famous queen in ancient Japan), or something else."

That was his last word. He bowed and made an exit. I was awestruck by the revelation and could not move for a few seconds. I felt I had grasped a very important essence of the philosophy of Shinto.

I knew that deities were named after people, but I had never suspected until that fateful day that this principle applied also to Amaterasu, *the* most important goddess in Japanese mythology. As the young Shinto priest had suggested, Amaterasu most certainly had a name when she was human, which is now lost. After this wonderful woman passed away, people reflected on her life. They came up with the name Amaterasu, which literally means "Radiant Heaven." Amaterasu, when she was a living, flesh and blood person, must have been a woman who made people around her happy, who brought light into people's hearts. That was why the world became dark when Amaterasu hid herself in Heaven's Cave Door. How fitting, then, was the name Amaterasu (Radiant Heaven), to commemorate this wonderful person!

In modern times, the tradition of humans becoming deities appears to have ceased, although it is customary for Buddhists to give the deceased a *kaimyo* (posthumous Buddhist name). Today, it is customary to have a commemorative plate describing the list of kaimyo of the deceased family members in the butsudan. Being fondly remembered in this way by members of your family and your close friends means that a nagomi is possible, even with the inescapable finality of death. This is also true in other cultures, where people remember the deceased by dedicating a park bench to them, visiting their grave, or simply having photos of their loved one. These loving tributes are the ultimate in the nagomi of life.

CHAPTER 9

Nagomi of Society

So far, we've explored the nagomi of food, self, relationships, health, learning, creativity, and life. All these aspects come together to make up our society.

As I have already mentioned, Japan has incorporated elements of many different cultures within its society. In the process of modernization, there was an enormous influx of Western culture entering the country. It is the way of nagomi that has made it possible for Japan to successfully integrate these aspects of Western culture without losing its distinct identity. Indeed, in Japan, we use the saying *batakusai* (which means "smells of butter") to indicate when something Western has too much influence. When something is too batakusai, it threatens to overbalance the way of nagomi. For example, satirical comedy dealing with current affairs has not entered Japan, despite the great tradition of comedy exemplified by rakugo (which we looked at in chapter 4). Liberal arts education, based on the initiatives of the students, is hard to introduce, as Japanese schools are obsessed with paper test scores. Investigative journalism, independent of governmental information sources, is a rarity in Japanese media.

Cultural assimilation is admittedly a delicate act of balance. In Japan, nagomi of society means that decisions are made in view of the various elements that affect human life. It is simply not enough to maximize profit; even if something appears inefficient on the surface, that could well be because it is the result of a detailed and sophisticated balancing act. Just like the metaphor of the magic carpet, we look to achieve balance between a variety of elements in order to make sustainable economic developments. In other words, we seek nagomi.

Here's an example of the nagomi of society in action. Although Eiichi Shibusawa was a short man, just 4 feet 9 inches (150 cm) tall, he was a giant in terms of his achievements. Within just a few decades, he founded many companies that eventually grew into economic mammoths, such as Mizuho Bank, Tokio Marine, the Imperial Hotel, Tokyo Stock Exchange, Kirin Beer,

Sapporo Beer, Jiji Press, Kyodo Press, and Nippon Yusen. In addition, Shibusawa was responsible for the establishment of Hitotsubashi University and the Japanese Red Cross Society. Shibusawa is often dubbed the "Father of Japan's capitalism," something that will be commemorated when he becomes the face featured on Japan's ten-thousand-yen banknotes in 2024, replacing the current face, Yukichi Fukuzawa.

When you study the way Shibusawa went about his work, it's clear to see he understood that, even in the face of merciless economic competition, it is essential to apply a principle of nagomi. Shibusawa used to claim that the purpose of a private company was not to maximize profits, but to strike a balance between well-being and profit not only for the capitalists, but for the employees, customers, and society at large. In his best-known book, *Rongo and Soroban* ("Analects of Confucius and the Abacus"), Shibusawa argued that it was important to harmonize ethics and profits by giving private wealth back to society at large. In this way, he believed, it is possible to fully develop the economy and also make the society as a whole richer.

Shibusawa's words might sound like an idyllic and even unrealistic fable today—when greedy founders and CEOs possess unreasonably large portions of the world's wealth. However, we need to have a clear vision of the ideal, even if we are trying to muddle through a field of unkind realities, and Shibusawa's words and philosophy can offer a model of excellence to strive for.

It is also important to realize that Shibusawa is not an isolated case in the long history of Japanese economics. In the Edo era, before the modernization of Japan, many people who struck it rich expressed similar views. The unique value of Shibusawa's philosophy is that he applied Japan's long-held ethics of sharing and community awareness at the time of nation-building, which means that his legacy is felt through the whole spectrum of the Japanese economy, through the ethics and ways of life that people still follow. For sure, greedy styles of capitalism have entered Japan, but they have never occupied a central position. Some economists in Japan have preached the importance of maximizing profits for the shareholders, but they have never captured the heart of the average Japanese person. For the majority of people, Shibusawa's words make more sense than the sermons of avaricious CEOs who stress the importance of always aiming to maximize profits. Indeed, there is plenty of wisdom to be found in the Japanese style of capitalism, as exemplified by Shibusawa. This is where nagomi comes in.

Once, my colleague in the social sciences, Dr. Anna Froese, visited me from Berlin. She was interested in studying the social significance of ikigai, the key concept in my previous book. We had a discussion in the lab, and then I took her to an izakaya (remember, this is a Japanese tavern) in the heart of the Gotanda district in Tokyo, where my lab is located. The place was full of company employees from nearby corporations. Due to the gender bias still prevalent in Japanese society, roughly 80 percent of the customers were men. Anna asked me about the customers, and I explained that they were employees from the same company. It is customary, I told her, for Japanese salarymen to go to an izakaya and open up to each other, complaining about their workplace, boss, family, health, etc. Eating, drinking, and sharing woes at the izakaya is one of the greatest pastimes of Japanese company employees, and is regarded as a fantastic way to release stress as well as reaffirm and solidify personal bonds.

Anna looked surprised. I, for my part, was surprised that Anna was surprised. In German workplaces, Anna said, the typical employee would not dream of doing such a thing. There is serious competition among employees to get promoted, and German business-people would not think of revealing weakness to their colleagues, she told me. This revealed to me one of the great cultural differences between Japan and Germany. It also told me that the spirit of nagomi permeates the life of workers in Japanese companies.

The Japanese have traditionally regarded the workplace as a family to which one belonged. There is a sense of coziness and togetherness, with an undertone of a "you scratch my back and I'll scratch yours" sentiment. It's no surprise, then, that employees confide in one another, and an izakaya is a great place for people to expose their vulnerabilities with the accompaniment of sake. Interestingly, for a long time now, this cozy atmosphere has been the target of criticism, not only from other international businesses, but also from Japanese people themselves. The downside of the family-like environment of Japanese companies is that they can be a hotbed for inefficiency, the argument goes. There should be more competitiveness, and employees should discipline themselves more, they say.

These people are disregarding Shibusawa's belief that it is not imperative for companies to maximize profits. The name of the game is something more complicated and richer, encompassing a whole spectrum of human nature. The implicit understanding is that nagomi is important above anything else. It is the most valuable thing to have a feeling of nagomi among those who work for a company, so nagomi, rather than profits or efficiency, should be maximized.

The case of nagomi in Japanese companies is interesting. It tells us that when something appears to be far from optimum, there might be an underlying principle of nagomi at work—and this goes beyond economic activities.

Politics might not be everyone's cup of tea, but it affects our everyday lives and our long-term future.

Politics has an impact on how we live and grow, and ultimately determines how happy we can be in the long run. The mission statement of Japanese politics has always been that of achieving the nagomi of society. This has been true in both domestic and international politics.

Japan is a democracy where members of the parliament are elected by free election, but, compared to countries such as the United States and the United Kingdom or even some Asian neighbors such as South Korea and Taiwan, Japanese politics has seen fewer changes of government through election results, with the Liberal Democratic Party (LDP) having been in power for most of the time since the end of the Second World War. The reason for these relatively few changes of government in Japan is a bit of a mystery, not only for people outside Japan but also for the Japanese people themselves. Some, including myself, have wondered if the long rule of the LDP and its coalitions might suggest an immaturity in Japanese democracy. However, with nagomi in mind, one might arrive at a different conclusion.

Perhaps the LDP's success can be explained by the fact that it practices a politics of nagomi. It is not uncommon for the LDP to negotiate, sometimes behind closed doors, with the opposition parties about policies; in effect, some of the things that the opposition wanted (better social welfare, raising of the minimum wage, etc.) have been brought to pass by the LDP. Other parties were then not in opposition as such, but instead functioned as complementary groups on the political scene. In terms of policy negotiations and parliamentary sessions, Japanese opposition parties have been in nagomi with the ruling party. There are even rumors that the Chief Cabinet Secretary's secret funds, amounting to more than a million dollars per month, have been partially used for negotiations with the opposition parties. As with any political rumor, this is probably true. These secret funds, set up as a means to run the country smoothly, have been used for the nagomi between the ruling party and the opposition parties.

From a Western point of view, nagomi between the ruling and opposition parties might sound like corruption, but it isn't when you really think about it. Consider a political system where two major parties alternately form the government. This might sound like a good idea–certainly better than one-party rule–but it means that at any given time, about half of the population feels left out, as the political party they voted for is not in government. In the United States, for example, supporters of the Democratic or Republican Parties at any one time feel excluded from the political process, depending on which candidate happens to be in the White House at any point. The same is true in the United Kingdom for Conservative and Labour voters. However, it is certainly true that in these countries, people with opposing ideas often find it difficult to even talk to each other in this post-truth and echo-chamber era.

Nagomi can be a wonderful guiding principle to direct one's decisions and behavior in society–in the political arena and beyond. Just as it shows that the maximization of profits is not the sole goal of economic activity, it is not the single purpose of politics to pursue the policy of the ruling party only, while crushing the opposition. In a world where political, economic, and social issues are becoming increasingly complex, it is important to consider any opposing values with nagomi in mind. By applying nagomi, we can mitigate conflict and nurture more sustainable and productive policies. Even when a particular viewpoint appears to be absolutely correct at the time, it might be bad, even disastrous, to pursue that ideal beyond nagomi. It always makes sense to apply nagomi and seek harmony between many different elements when considering a political position.

To find a demonstration of the sustainability brought about by applying nagomi to society, you need look no further than the Japanese Imperial Family. In Japan, the political stance (if any) of the Imperial Family has been that of pure nagomi. In the long history of Japan, the Imperial Family has stayed away from forming any pacts with the ruling political forces, no matter how strong and dominant they might have seemed at the time. Instead of becoming too closely associated with the powers that have come and gone, the emperor has always acted as a moderating agent, giving the final authority and legitimacy to the samurai or shogun powers that might emerge as the ruling force at any time. As a consequence the Imperial House of Japan is the longest-surviving hereditary monarchy in the world.

Nagomi also makes practical sense when we go about our personal relationships in our everyday lives. As I mentioned earlier, the Western approach is sometimes based too much on a model of confrontation, rather than nagomi. You might think that it is important to defeat your opponent, but the way of nagomi would rather suggest that you should not make an enemy of anybody in the first place. When you speak badly about a person, that person will naturally be hurt. They will be less inclined to collaborate with you in the future or to regard you as a possible friend. We are living in an increasingly connected world, with social networks creating a society where everyone is on average six or fewer social connections away from everyone else, so it is not a good idea to quarrel with anyone too much.

That doesn't mean you can't make your opinions known; it just means we should all try not to be unfair or unkind. In keeping with the spirit of nagomi, we should seek to collaborate and maintain a friendly relationship even with our fiercest opponent. Identity politics don't do society much good if rivalries between the identities are pushed forward too much; it is always worthwhile to try to see the viewpoint of the other side, so that you become a mitigator rather than a fighter. Practicing nagomi with your enemy can be one of the most rewarding and sustainable practices in your life. If you master the art of nagomi, you can keep growing and prospering, and embrace the great diversity of the world.

There is increasing urgency in the need to understand and apply nagomi in society at every level as the world moves toward a more confrontational mood, and clashes between opposing ideologies start to look inevitable. Even when a particular viewpoint appears to be absolutely correct at a particular time, it might be bad, even disastrous, for our lives to pursue that ideal beyond what the way of nagomi would advise. Many social experiments aiming to implement an ideal society have resulted in hell. It always makes sense to apply nagomi when considering a particular political position.

Japan has traditionally occupied a middle ground when it comes to confrontation. There have been deeply regrettable points, however—as in the Second

World War—when Japan has been a militarily aggressive nation and the way of nagomi was lost, with devastating consequences for Japan and its neighboring nations.

More recently, when it comes to facing human rights abuses and oppressive government practices, Japan has been typically slow in making protests and imposing necessary sanctions. Given this track record, some lament the human rights awareness of the Japanese government and its people. These criticisms are at least partially justified. By various measures, progress toward better gender equality in the country is in shambles. Japanese television and newspapers have long been criticized for the closed mindset of the *kisha* club that excludes independent journalists and foreign media from open access, resulting in less freedom of the press compared to other economically developed nations.

So, like every nation, Japan has its problems. It has in recent times, however, achieved meaningful relationships with other countries, some of which have political systems the Japanese government might not necessarily agree with.

In the world today, we are experiencing frictions between alternative and competing ways of organizing society and of underlying values. In the few years after the fall of the Berlin Wall, an optimistic view of the future of human civilization was prevalent, in which it was hoped that the world would witness a triumphant and prosperous convergence of parliamentary democracy and a free market. In 1992, Francis Fukuyama famously declared in his book *The End of History and the Last Man* that the competition between alternative ways to manage human society was over. Recent developments, however, have shown that Fukuyama was wrong, or at least, that the jury is still out.

The values expressed by the governments of some nations seem far apart, so much so that there appears to be no chance of compromise. Rival governments all seem to believe that they alone have a blueprint for a sustainable future, and a compromise between opposing ideologies is unlikely. This is precisely when the spirit of the nagomi of society should come to the rescue, in order to make the future of human civilization truly in harmony and sustainable. It may be a cliché, but people from different nations are all human, dreaming the same dreams and aspiring to the same achievements. There should be ways for nations of different ideologies to coexist in harmony. If the people of nations that hold different ideologies could all smile together, that would be one of the most creative instances of the nagomi of society toward a peaceful world.

Here, it is important to stress that keeping a nagomi does not necessarily mean submission, conformity, or compromising on your dearly held principles. The nagomi of society means acknowledging differences and admitting and recognizing each other's position in the world, which has been formed over long years through complex dynamics of culture and history. Too often, there is a tendency to think that one person or side has the "right" answer while the other is mistaken. The way of nagomi is letting others go their own way, even when you feel that you are right beyond any reasonable doubt.

It is interesting that Japanese society has always been relatively free of any dominant ideologies. Historically, whenever an ideology appeared to be gaining momentum, there was either systemic or spontaneous resistance in a bid to maintain the nagomi of society. An example of this is how Christianity was received and then rejected in Japan in the Middle Ages. The samurai warriors saw the work of the missionaries to convert the people of Japan and worried that their influence would radically impact and even destroy the indigenous cultures. Seen from this perspective, the harsh rejection of Christianity, as depicted in Shusaku Endo's masterful novel *Silence*, was perhaps an inevitable and regrettable by-product of the maintenance of nagomi.

Elements of Christianity can still be found in Japan today, however. In Japan, there isn't too much friction between different religions. It is customary for a Japanese person to have a Christian-style wedding, go to a Shinto shrine on New Year's Day for a ritual called *hatsumoude* ("the first visit to the shrine in the year" and, for many, the only visit), and have a Buddhist funeral. For many in Japan, there is no problem with adopting the traditions of different religions. A Christian wedding is considered to be more romantic, a visit to the Shinto shrine on the New Year's Day resonates with the feeling of starting afresh with a blank page in your life, and the solemnity of a funeral is best expressed in the traditional Buddhist manner.

This might appear flippant and perhaps disrespectful to people who are very religious, but it is true that Japan has successfully become almost free of religious or other civil conflicts. I regard this as one of the ultimate achievements of the nagomi of society in Japan.

In life, it is important to keep your curiosity active, and learn and absorb new influences. On the other hand, striking a balance is necessary so that society remains stable. Nagomi is not about ideologies, left or right, progressive or conservative, or religious or secular. Nagomi is about how to maintain balance in life, which is the most precious thing. When carefully tuned, nagomi can be used in a way that will promote both diversity and individual freedom so we can share our cultures and coexist peacefully together.

CHAPTER 10

Nagomi of Nature

When we consider the natural world, it is useful to keep the Japanese tradition of *kintsugi* in mind. Kintsugi is the ancient technique of mending broken wares by applying *urushi* (a substance that derives from the sap of the Chinese lacquer tree), gold power, and other materials to the cracks. The practice and principle of kintsugi embraces, rather than rejects, defects in the makeup of things, and can be applied to almost anything in life. You don't throw away a chipped cup or a broken bowl; you take great care of them and treat them as indispensable fragments to be connected back together. In the spirit of kintsugi, one would not abandon the Earth just because it has been affected and damaged by human activities.

The Japanese people have one of the most all-encompassing views of life. In the Buddhist tradition, plants are believed to have a soul, and their lives have

always been central to the spirituality of Japan. In today's world, with its technologies and big city lights, some people see the Earth's environment as dispensable. Nothing is further from the truth.

Ikebana is the Japanese art of flower arranging, and it has been carried out by the Ikenobo family in the heart of the ancient city of Kyoto for more than five hundred years. Senko Ikenobo is the first female *iemoto* (head) in the long history of ikebana at the House of Ikenobo. When asked about the significance of ikebana, the Ikenobo master invariably cites a reverence for all living things, and a prayer for the salvation of their souls. Ikebana flower arrangement is a form of prayer for all living things.

Naturally, in order to make ikebana, one has to cut flowers, shortening their precious lives. However, by doing so, ikebana can make the flowers, leaves, and twigs attain a more beautiful state than would have been possible if left alone. The physical beautification of the plants thus spiritually ameliorates them. Ikebana is an application of the way of nagomi (nagomido), going beyond the borders between species to welcome plants as soulmates of human beings.

In nature, as in all walks of life, it is important to strike a balance between different perspectives in a beautiful nagomi. When it comes to the endeavor of balancing human activities with the natural world, it is important to consider the Japanese concept of *satoyama*. Satoyama describes the borders between *sato* (human habitat) and *yama* (mountain), and so it is where civilization and nature meet and result in a beautiful harmony. Throughout Japan, you can find satoyama along the borders between plains and mountains, or between the valleys and flatlands. Indeed, a satoyama is a uniquely Japanese idea about how to establish a nagomi between human activities and nature.

A satoyama is very beautiful to see, and once you observe a good example of it in action, the impression stays with you forever, providing an image of what life should look like with nagomi, and providing inspiration for the nagomi of health.

The idea of satoyama is wonderfully depicted in Hayao Miyazaki's film *My Neighbor Totoro*. The rural setting in which the two little girls, Satsuki and Mei, roam and go on adventures is a typical example of satoyama. Although Miyazaki is characteristically ambiguous about the location that inspired the film, an educated guess would point to Tokorozawa, a suburban town in the area of Saitama, north of Tokyo. The daughter of Miyazaki's friend is said to have mispronounced Tokorozawa as "Totorozawa," providing the name of the big creature in the film. In particular, the Sayamakyuryo green hills spreading from Tokorozawa to Tokyo are widely regarded as the satoyama depicted in the film. Today, there is a National Trust movement that is trying to preserve the Sayamakyuryo green hills, and Miyazaki is a patron.

As the film suggests, a satoyama environment lends itself to human life; it is the human activities that make the various lives in satoyama rich and diverse. In the West, there is a tendency to think of nature as best when left alone by humans. This is understandable in a way, and everyone would agree that a pristine primordial forest is something to be valued and cherished in its own right. However, satoyama provides an alternative approach, which states that in fact, rather than unilaterally destroying the natural world, human activity can sometimes increase the biodiversity and the emergence of unique habitats and ecosystems. In a typical satoyama environment, the harmonious coexistence of nature and civilization could go on for centuries.

A wonderful example of the unique ecological system that a satoyama nurtures can be found near Japan's biggest lake, Biwa, in the Takashima region in Shiga prefecture. Here, there is an intricately balanced network of ecological systems involving greenery, water, vegetation, and various other life-forms that inhabit those spaces. Most famously, carp swim in the water near the local residents' houses. In fact, they actually swim into them. Kitchens in these houses in the Takashima region are equipped with waterways that meander from the natural water to pools located right in their kitchens. For residents of the region, it is an everyday thing to see carp swimming in water pools in a corner of their kitchen. This image, of carp swimming around in a kitchen, is so beautiful, symbolic of what satoyama stands for.

The benefit of having fish swimming around in your kitchen goes beyond that of pure aesthetics. It has practical advantages, too. You can put your dishes in the pool after you have eaten and the fish will come and eat scraps off the surface, serving as your co-diners as well as your cleaners. The carp appear to be particularly fond of leftover rice.

The nagomi of the lives of both people and carp is realized by intelligence, passion, and dexterity, in the form of *teire*. Teire literally means "putting hands" or, more loosely, "continuous human care." Teire is considered to be an important and necessary part of our role in preserving and protecting the natural world. Japanese gardens are beautifully maintained by the teire of the craftspeople who serve them. From amateur gardeners to the professionals working on its UNESCO World Heritage sites, Japan is a great country of teire. Without teire, the maintenance of forests, gardens, and even bonsai trees (which I will discuss in more detail shortly) is impossible.

In essence, teire is a nagomi between artificial and natural processes. If left only to nature, the beautiful sight of carp in kitchen pools would not have been possible. These waterways that enable carp to swim seamlessly between the natural and developed worlds are a product of nagomi created by teire.

Without satoyama achieved through teire, the very existence of nature can come under threat. As a child, I was fond of nature. I particularly loved butterflies and used to be an amateur entomologist, exploring various satoyama areas in the name of research. I reported what I found at the local science fair and received some awards. I have a vivid memory of one species in particular: the *Niphanda fusca*, a small black butterfly with elegant spot patterns on the ventral side (underside) of its wings. This butterfly is found in areas where human activity has resulted in open grasslands flanking sunlit forests. This unique species, found only in East Asian regions including Japan and Korea, feeds on sweet liquid secreted from the ant *Camponotus japonicus*, or Japanese carpenter ant.

Both insects can thrive only in the satoyama environment, where the effects of human activity and nature mingle and merge. Sadly, the *Niphanda fusca* population is now rapidly decreasing, and the species is registered as endangered on the Regional Red List of the Ministry of the Environment in Japan. The main reason for the demise of this species is the vanishing of the satoyama environment, due to the shift in human society and subsequent disappearance of traditional activities such as farming, the collecting of firewood, and the cutting of undergrowth in and around forests. All these activities are labor-intensive and difficult to maintain in a time of challenging economic circumstances.

There are other endangered species unique to the satoyama environment. *Fabriciana nerippe* is a magnificent orange butterfly indigenous to grasslands maintained through farming and pasturing. Another species, *Shijimiaeoides divinus*, an elegant, small blue butterfly, thrives in grasslands flanking farmlands and abandoned rice fields and is endangered, too, due to changes in farming and land use patterns. The fact that these once-common species have reduced greatly in numbers is largely considered to be the result of change in human activity.

It is incredible that so many endangered species rely on satoyama environments nurtured at the borders between natural and artificial environments. The same is true of other insect species (besides butterflies), mammals, birds, fish, plants, and fungi, which were once nurtured and are now endangered by the disappearance of satoyama environments. Interaction with humans can create unique habitats in nature. In general, nagomi is an awareness of the networks of interaction in the ecological system, and satoyama is one beautiful example of it.

One final example of nagomi and satoyama as guiding principles for fostering a harmonious coexistence between humans and the natural world is the botanical art of bonsai.

Bonsai originated in China as the art of *penjing* or *penzai*, and, like many other things native to China, evolved to become its own tradition in Japan. Today, bonsai is popular within Japan as well as all over the world. In the Imperial Palace in Tokyo, there are about six hundred bonsai trees, encompassing ninety different species and showcasing the finest in the genre. Some of these trees are hundreds of years old, and this is down to a continuous teire.

Teire is an essential aspect of the nurturing of bonsai trees, as, to maintain these miniature trees, you must clip and prune the leaves. One bonsai artist said that by bending the trunks and boughs of the small trees, he was imitating the effects of wind and snow in the wild and thus reproducing the workings of Mother Earth in the tree's small pot. This is a wonderful distillation of teire achieving satoyama, and it demonstrates the perfect nagomi of nature.

Conclusion

Let us look again at the five pillars of nagomi:

1. Maintain happy relationships with your loved ones, even if you disagree with them.

2. Learn new things while always staying true to yourself.

3. Find a sense of peace in whatever you are doing.

4. Mix and blend unlikely components to strike a harmonious balance.

5. Have a greater understanding of the Japanese philosophy of life.

Now, having read the book, how do these pillars of nagomi appear to you?

- Are you more inclined to focus on nurturing happy relationships with your loved ones, without necessarily agreeing with them on everything?

- Do you feel more able to learn new things but stay true to yourself?

- Does the idea of finding a sense of peace in whatever you do seem more like something you could do, or work toward?

- Do you feel that you could experiment with blending unlikely components and that you may—by doing so—find a harmonious balance?

- Does the concept of nagomi seem perhaps more understandable and relevant to you than it did?

- I hope you can close this book with a good understanding of the way of nagomi. I wish you all the peace and harmonious balance nagomi may bring.

- May the nagomi be with you!

Glossary

Batakusai: this literally means "smells of butter" and is used to indicate when something Western has too much influence, such as satirical comedies

Butsudan: a Buddhist shrine to which families pay their respects

Chanko: the traditional way of preparing food for sumo wrestlers, so that they can gain weight while still maintaining good health.

En: it can be translated as fate or connection (like family or a loved one)

Gaman: a concept related to perseverance and self-restraint, which is one of the most important premises of Zen Buddhism

Getsukoyoku: moonlight bathing

Hanami: the appreciation of flowers

Harahachibu: literally translates as "stomach 80 percent," it is the idea that you should stop eating before you are completely full so you can avoid overeating

Hashiri: this refers to the start of the season, when new ingredients start to fill the market

Hatsumoude: the word to describe the first visit to a Shinto shrine on New Year's Day

Ichigo ichie: the concept of treasuring a moment in time. It can be translated as "once in a lifetime" and it reminds people to cherish any experience they may share with others, such as a Japanese tea ceremony

Ichiju issai: a system of creating a meal, based on one soup, one dish

Ikebana: the traditional art of flower arranging

Ikigai: the Japanese philosophy that helps you to find mindfulness and joy in everything you do

Izakaya: a traditional Japanese tavern

Kaiseki: this describes the harmonious balance of ingredients in dishes

Kaisuiyoku: bathing in an ocean

Kawaii: this translates roughly as "cute" in English, but its meaning changes slightly depending on the context

Kintsugi: the ancient technique of mending broken wares by applying *urushi* (a substance that derives from the sap of the Chinese lacquer tree), gold powder, and other materials to the cracks

Kokugaku: the study of Japanese history

Kounaichoumi: cooking in the mouth

Mono no aware: the pathos of things

Nagori: the end of the season, when ingredients become less available

Nikkoyoku: sunbeam bathing

Okazu: an accompaniment

Omakase: chef's choice

Onsenyoku: bathing in a hot spring

Rakugo: traditional theater where a single storyteller assumes the role of different characters, often in stories involving conflict

Ryokan: a traditional Japanese inn

Sado: the way of tea

Sakana: an old word to describe any kind of food that goes well with sake

Sakari: the middle of the season, when ingredients are at their tastiest

Satoyama: this describes the borders between *sato* (human habitat) and *yama* (mountain), and so it is where civilization and nature meet and result in a beautiful harmony. Throughout Japan, you can find *satoyama* along the borders between plains and mountains, or between the valleys and flatlands

Seiyu: voice actor

Sensei: teacher

Shakkei: this means borrowed scenery. For example, the Genkyuen Garden in the city of Hikone is "borrowing" the views of adjacent Hikone Castle, a samurai-period masterpiece designated as a National Treasure

Shinrin-yoku: a relatively new word, coined in 1982 by Tomohide Akiyama, the chief of the Ministry of Forestry at that time, meaning forest bathing (i.e., being in nature)

Shodo: calligraphy

Shokado: an elegantly presented bento box

Shokuiku: food education

Sodoku: the traditional way to start learning (not to be confused with sudoku)

Teire: literally means "putting hands" or, more loosely, "continuous human care." *Teire* is considered to be an important and necessary part of our role in preserving and protecting the natural world

Tokowaka: literally translates as "forever young"

Tsumami: describes the range of dishes specially conceived and developed to accompany sake. It can also refer to food that can be accompanied by other alcoholic drinks such as beer, whisky and wine. One can say, for example, that edamame is a perfect *tsumami* for beer, or that cheese is an excellent *tsumami* for wine

Ukiyo: the floating world, which refers to the importance of the ephemeral in Japanese life, like the appreciation of cherry blossoms in the spring

Wabi sabi: the acceptance of transience and imperfection

Waka: a type of poetry in classical Japanese literature

Wayochu: refers to the cooking styles originating in Japan (*wa*), the West (*yo*) and China (*chu*), and it represents the major genre of foods available in modern Japan

Yoku: a generic word to describe bathing, but it can refer to immersing yourself in any ambient atmosphere

Yomihitoshirazu: a way to describe a work created anonymously

Zatsudan: a Japanese word for describing "small talk." *Zatsu* refers to the rich diversity of topics within a conversation and *dan* is to do with the colorful narratives that are captured in people's idiosyncratic conversations

Zen Buddhism: a faith and religious discipline that centers the contemplation of the meaning of life

ABOUT THE AUTHOR

KEN MOGI is a neuroscientist, writer, and broadcaster based in Tokyo. He has published more than thirty papers on cognitive science and neuroscience, and over one hundred books in Japan covering popular science, essay, criticism, and self-help. His books have sold close to one million copies. He is also the author of *Awakening Your Ikigai*.

qualiajournal.blogspot.com | ⓘ **qualiaken** | **kenmogi**

ALSO AVAILABLE BY KEN MOGI

"*Awakening Your Ikigai* is really quite a delightful look at sometimes mystifying Japanese traditions."

—*The New York Times Book Review*

Ikigai is a Japanese phenomenon commonly understood as "your reason to get up in the morning." In this book, Ken Mogi introduces five pillars of ikigai to help you make the most of each day and become your most authentic self.

Paper over Boards

$16.95 US • 224 pages • 978-1-61519-475-9